D1304409

Elizabeth Taylor

Elizabeth Taylor

Sheridan Morley

PAVILION
MICHAEL JOSEPH

For Hugo, Alexis and Juliet

This edition published in Great Britain in 1989 by
PAVILION BOOKS LIMITED
196 Shaftesbury Avenue, London WC2H 8JL
in association with Michael Joseph Limited
27 Wrights Lane, London W8 5TZ

First hardback edition published in 1988

Designed by Fraser Morgan

A CIP catalogue record for this book is
available from the British Library

ISBN 1 85145 437 3 pbk
ISBN 1 85145 051 3 hbk

Library of Congress Catalog Card Number 89–83705

10 9 8 7 6 5 4 3 2

Printed and bound in Great Britain
by Butler & Tanner Ltd, Frome

Contents

The Last Star   6

The Kid who had Nothing   18

Engaged to be Engaged   32

Miss Rich Bitch   48

Mother Superior   64

Todd Almighty   80

Scandal Time   98

Serpent of the Nile   116

The Burtons   138

Mother Courage in Sables   166

Filmography   184

Acknowledgements   192

The Last Star

'MGM taught me how to be a star more than forty years ago, and I have never really known how to be anything else'

We were in a pub just off Flask Walk in Hampstead: it must have been some time in the early summer of 1966. Elizabeth Taylor was then thirty-four, and into the third year of her fifth marriage, though her first to Richard Burton; together they were just off to Italy to make *The Taming of the Shrew* for Franco Zeffirelli. As a double act, they were then at the height of their fame and fortune; they had made *Cleopatra*, *The VIPs*, *The Sandpiper* and most notably *Who's Afraid of Virginia Woolf?* within five years, and there was as yet no sign that a remarkable run of commercial and sometimes even critical fortune was to end somewhat abruptly after the *Shrew*.

Though what I now recall most clearly about that Hampstead pub lunch was a long and surprising conversation with Taylor, I had not in fact gone there to interview her at all. I was there to write a magazine profile of Burton, largely because I had noticed that within a much publicized Hollywood-royalty partnership, a road-show version of the one-time Oliviers, he alone had managed to keep a separate career going as well. Where Taylor had done nothing without him professionally or privately since their fateful meeting on *Cleopatra* in the summer of 1961, Burton had managed to do some vastly better work without her: *The Night of the Iguana*, *The Spy Who Came in from the Cold* and above all *Becket*, as well as stage appearances of rather less distinction: as Hamlet on Broadway and Dr Faustus at the Oxford Playhouse.

True, Taylor had fleetingly appeared as the Helen whose face launched a thousand ships in the Oxford (and later screen) *Faustus*, but beyond that her interest in the stage was still minimal and I had begun to develop the theory that she should anyway have been playing Mephistopheles in that production, since it was surely she who had tempted Burton away from his classical stage career at Stratford and the Old Vic and into the vast and richer areas of Hollywood rubbish.

Waiting to talk to Richard that lunchtime (he had as usual double-booked himself and a rival hack was, as I arrived, already getting the familiar speech about how it was not impossible to be a rich film star and a great actor within the same career) I sat further along the bar and was

Audiences since *Lassie* had preferred her close to lovable pets, but MGM were still looking for an all-American girl; Taylor at fifteen in her second leading role as *Cynthia* (1947).

surprised to be joined after about ten minutes by Miss Taylor. I don't think she had actually intended to join me: she had just come into the pub to collect Burton for some afternoon venture, and finding him in mid-oration had, like me, settled down to wait. I didn't like to point out that I was waiting for him too, since that clearly was going to make her wait even longer. On the other hand it seemed curiously inefficient journalistically to sit entirely alone at the end of a bar with the most famous and bankable film star in world history and not say anything at all, so having established that she didn't want a drink, I reminded her that we had in fact met fleetingly twice before; first in California at the very end of the 1940s when she was at the height of her *National Velvet* teenage career and I was about ten and living with my grandmother Gladys Cooper, already a dowager leader of that Hollywood Raj of expatriate English actors which Taylor had joined as a wartime evacuee from London and for which both women had made *The White Cliffs of Dover* in 1944; and then back in England about five years later when she had made *Beau Brummell* with my father.

8

That proved a less than wonderful opening gambit: apart from her lifelong friend Roddy McDowall, who was also in *White Cliffs* and had, like her, started out in Hollywood as the child star of movies essentially devoted to four-legged characters, Taylor had found few allies among a comparatively ancient English colony in Beverly Hills, and most of her memories of English actors now centred on an unhappy marriage to one of the last junior officers and gentlemen of that particular Raj, Michael Wilding.

Talking about her recent career proved not a lot easier: she understandably had not much cared for the way *The Sandpiper* or *The VIPs* had turned out, found *Virginia Woolf* a lot better but mentally and physically demoralizing, and was now not much looking forward to 'all the Shakespeare' which she rightly guessed was to be at the heart of *The Taming of the Shrew* and probably difficult to learn.

For a while, therefore, it was much like a conversation with minor royalty: questions were answered efficiently but bleakly, with a kind of radiant boredom. Twenty years on from there, when sons of that other Queen Elizabeth began marrying into the ranks of ranging Sloanes, I suddenly realized what a wonderful consort this upper-middle-class art dealer's daughter would have made for anyone about third in line to a surviving throne. Indeed if anyone were ever to take part in a screen life of Princess Margaret or Michael, then it should surely be Taylor. A career of incessant waving at crowds of onlookers, uttering publicly the often undistinguished speeches of others and getting photographed from increasingly undesirable angles cannot be so very different, whether it is lived in America or Switzerland or a small palace in Kensington.

But it still comes as something of a shock to realize that Elizabeth Taylor, the last female superstar created by the Hollywood publicity machine before it broke apart in the mid-1960s, is so very unlike all of the others. Or nearly all. Unlike Katharine Hepburn, she had no real talent for acting; unlike Marilyn Monroe, she was not especially or uniquely loved by the camera; unlike Joan Crawford or Bette Davis, she had no burning desire to succeed at any

'My troubles all
started because
I had the body
of a woman
and the
emotions of a
child.'

cost; Taylor couldn't sing like Dietrich or dance like
Ginger Rogers; she didn't have legs like Grable or the
urchin appeal of Garland; she didn't have a look like
Lauren Bacall's or a recognizable comic gift like Carole
Lombard's; she wasn't a child star like Shirley Temple or
a veteran legend like Lillian Gish. It is only when you get
to the greatest pre-war star of them all that you find
shared territory: if Taylor is like anyone in movies, she is
like Greta Garbo. That same curiously blank expression,
the constant feeling that she'd rather be anywhere than in
this particular film at this particular time, and yet an
absolute technical mastery of her medium: what Garbo
had been for the 1920s and 30s, Taylor was for the 1940s
and 50s and 60s.

And if one writes about her now, aged fifty-five, in the
past tense it is not because her career is over: after a
difficult time both privately and professionally she re-
emerged in the late 1980s as a born-again legend, and will
doubtless carry on into her seventies as one of those

indomitable old Hollywood survivors who achieve in smaller and flashier roles the Oscars often denied at the height of their powers. The reason one writes about her in the past is that her career as a studio creation has been ended by a changing movie world: nobody, not even Elizabeth Taylor, could now set out to be Elizabeth Taylor with any real chance of success. Stars just don't come like that any more, because the skies have gone dark: you didn't get to be Elizabeth Taylor on videotape, you got to be Elizabeth Taylor in a cinema where the screen was the size of a small car park.

But at the time of our accidental Hampstead encounter twenty years ago she was, as the leading half of The Burtons, more than fifty per cent of a pop group second only at that time to The Beatles in public acclaim and interest; and as my attempts at some sort of conversation about her Hollywood or immediate past withered away in the kind of amiable neglect that characterizes conversations with the Duchess of Gloucester at royal garden parties, the two of us could not help overhearing the interview that Burton was still giving further along the bar. By this time he had got over the bit about his ongoing plans to play *King Lear* on stage and screen, done the

Spencer Tracy's favourite daughter in *Father of the Bride*; and in reality as Mrs Nicky Hilton.

11

The changing faces of Elizabeth Taylor: a studio publicity shot from 1951; replacing Vivien Leigh in *Elephant Walk* (1954); as Gloria Wandrous in *Butterfield 8* (1960); and at the beginning of her first Burton marriage in 1963.

quote (which he variously attributed to Olivier, Gielgud and Orson Welles) about it being impossible to be great and rich and how he was going to disprove whoever it was first said it, and was moving on to the speech about how he was now teaching Taylor all there was to know about acting.

As if prompted by this, and in a tone of voice he could not fail to hear, Taylor then began giving what would have been a rival interview if only I'd had the intelligence to make a few notes. It was not Burton who had to teach *her* about acting, she remarked, but she who had been good enough to show him in which direction the bloody camera was pointing. Had he ever done anything even remotely notable on film before *Cleopatra*? If he was such a great and classical Shakespearian talent, what the hell had he been doing with Olivia de Havilland in *My Cousin Rachel* back in 1952? Since when had anyone appearing in *The Robe* acquired the right to teach acting? And another thing: if Burton wished to go back to the Vic, she would be the first to encourage him. It was not she who was standing in the way of his Shakespearian ambition, but his own desire to be as rich as she was.

In fact he had only just achieved that kind of parity in 1965 with *The Sandpiper*, which earned them each a

million dollars: for *Cleopatra*, as recently as 1963, when she was already at the million level, he was only on £100,000; and it was undoubtedly his relationship with her, off-camera as well as on, that now made him for 'one brief shining moment' (as he sang in *Camelot*) the most bankable of British stars.

Taylor simply wanted that acknowledged as part of the record: so far from Helen of Troy or Mephistopheles, she had in fact proved an agile career manager for the Burtons just as she always had for herself in the past. And I think it was then and there, in that Hampstead pub, that I began to realize there was something wrong with the conventional wisdom about Elizabeth Taylor.

Inside that overblown, headline-grabbing movie star, there has always existed an extremely powerful lady: though she lacks the emotional strength on camera of a Bette Davis or a Joan Crawford, she has always had their sense of total cinema. A child of the camera (both movie and paparazzi) who has had no stage life worth recalling except in terms of deep embarrassment, she grew up knowing only the power and the possibility of the lens. The way that Bernhardt first took to the stage, Taylor took to the screen: her best performances have always been massive and unashamed, and countless melodramas, from *Cat on a Hot Tin Roof* at the upper end of the scale, to *Butterfield 8* at rock bottom, have been made bearable and even unforgettable by her ability to invade and inhabit the screen as if it were all her personal property — which for a while, of course, it was.

Critical fashion is not currently on Taylor's side, and very often the greatest enemy to her own career has been her often more dramatic private life; but it needs now to be established that she belongs, with maybe less than half a dozen others in the entire history of Hollywood, to that rare pantheon of leading ladies who really were able to command the heights as well as the depths of cinema. It is more than doubtful whether any actress will ever again be as famous as was Elizabeth Taylor at her *Cleopatra* peak: but that very fame has tended to obscure a unique and intermittently remarkable acting career.

What we know about Elizabeth Taylor Hilton Wilding Todd Fisher Burton Burton Warner is that, now in her middle fifties, she has had seven marriages and six husbands, four of whom are already dead. The one she may well have loved most, Mike Todd, died violently in a plane crash barely a year after they married; two of the other men she most loved were gay and also died terrible deaths: Montgomery Clift of drink and drugs, and Rock Hudson of AIDS. She herself achieved Vatican blacklisting as 'an erotic vagrant', three children by Wilding and Todd plus one she adopted with Burton, two Oscars, seven nominations, nineteen operations, one near-terminal illness, five grandchildren, fifty feature films, one catastrophic Broadway flop (with Burton in his farewell stage appearance) and one so-so success there, about as much time in hospitals and clinics as under the arc lights of studios, a movie career that has veered on more than one occasion from the sublime to the ridiculous, and a private life that often reads like the worst kind of Hollywood paperback novel. Indeed one of my recurrent nightmares about Taylor is that she will one day star in a mini-series for American television based on a book about her Hollywood life by Jackie Collins. Much of Taylor's recent work has already been in soap operas, notably *General Hospital*, after a wide-screen career which seemed to grind to a halt in the late 1970s soon after the disastrous

Vienna filming of Stephen Sondheim's *A Little Night Music*. The Sondheim musical that Elizabeth Taylor ought to have played on stage and screen was his *Follies:*

I've been through Reno,
I've been through Beverly Hills,
And I'm here.
Reefers and vino,
Rest cures, religion and pills.
But I'm here . . .

I should have gone to an acting school,
That seems clear.
Still someone said, 'She's sincere',
So I'm here . . .

First you're another
Sloe-eyed vamp,
Then someone's mother,
Then you're camp. . .

On the occasion of her fifty-fourth birthday and her fifty-eighth film *There Must be a Pony* (1986).

Good times and bum times, she's seen them all and she's still here. Miss Taylor is not a lady much given to introspection, but she did once say something more than usually chilling in a conversation with the author Truman Capote. It was soon after she had married Burton for the first time, the best of times in fact: 'When you find what you've always wanted,' she told Capote, 'that's not where the beginning begins. That's where the end starts.' At which point we would do well to go back to where the beginning does in fact begin.

The Kid who had Nothing

'A beguilingly young newcomer named Elizabeth Taylor has emerged as one of the most outstanding discoveries of the year' *New York Journal* (1944)

The actress who once described herself, not altogether inaccurately or unreasonably, as 'Mother Courage in Sables' was born Elizabeth Rosemond Taylor in London on 27 February 1932 to American parents. Her father, Francis Taylor, came from a family of reasonably affluent Midwestern art dealers, and had moved to London in the late 1920s to set up an English branch of the business, one which was later to represent Augustus John among many other artists. Her mother, Sara Warmbrodt, had been born in Arkansas and started out as an actress under the name of Sara Sothern before marrying a childhood sweetheart and moving with him to the centre of his family's gallery business in St Louis.

Sara had enjoyed some success on the stage, and had played both on Broadway and on European tours with Edward Everett Horton's company, which also established a permanent home in Los Angeles for a while, so the world of Hollywood and indeed that of a touring actress was familiar to her long before the birth of her only daughter. But on her marriage in 1926 she had been more than happy to give it up, and when her only son was born three years later, the three Taylors moved from St Louis to London where Francis was detailed by his family to set up a gallery in Old Bond Street and buy European paintings new and old for the American market.

Because of their gallery, the Taylors almost immediately began to move in the more wealthy and fashionable circles of what was then still known as London society. An early client was Victor Cazalet, an extremely well-connected Conservative MP who took the Taylors to Buckingham Palace and ensured that little Elizabeth once got to dance before Princess Elizabeth, in about 1935, this being the earliest recorded meeting of the two Elizabethan queens.

Though Taylor's birth certificate reveals that the family were living in 1932 just over the border from Hampstead in Golders Green, their world was already that of Old Bond Street. Well financed by the family firm back in St Louis, and equipped now to do some shrewd art deals as both buyer and seller, Francis Taylor was able to send his young daughter to Madame Vacani's dancing school; Victor Cazalet gave her a pony to ride at the weekends the

A London childhood: with her mother and brother Howard in 1934; and the beginnings of *National Velvet*.

Taylors would spend on his country estate in Kent. Elizabeth herself later recalled 'the most idyllic childhood: there were hundreds of acres to roam over, and a farm of sorts, and my brother and I made pets of all the animals – pet rabbits, pet turtles, pet lambs, pet goats and pet chickens. It was my idea of real bliss, and I was a very small three when I was given my first pony by Victor Cazalet, who had become a sort of honorary godfather to me. The first time I climbed on her back, wearing a little organdie dress, she bucked me into a patch of stinging nettles, but they made me get right back on, and I hardly got off again until we left England.' The ride to *National Velvet* had already begun.

Taylor herself was later to look back on her dancing for Madame Vacani and royalty as an early indication of the direction her career would soon take ('It was a marvellous feeling on that stage – the isolation, the hugeness, the feeling of space and no end to space, the lights, the music – and then the applause bringing you back into focus, the noise rattling against your face . . .'). In fact she spent the next half-century almost totally off the stage, returning to it only for fleeting appearances with Burton in the late 1960s, and then again in the 1980s when it seemed her Hollywood career was over and even Broadway looked like a better option than the daytime soaps she was also sometimes to be found in by then.

For her first seven years Elizabeth Taylor led a somewhat charmed London and country life, weekending with the Cazalets and dancing for Vacani and going to school at the élite Byron House. Her mother was years later to remember a daughter 'already showing signs of hamminess', and Taylor herself recalled: 'Like my mother I always wanted to be an actress. I have always been constricted by shyness, and acting meant I could be at ease behind someone else's facade. When I was little I was always hiding from strangers behind my nurse's back with my finger in my mouth, but if someone ever asked me to dance, well I would have danced for hundreds of people quite happily.'

For Elizabeth and her elder brother, that charmed London life came to a rapid end in the spring of 1939. Like many Americans, including ambassador Joe Kennedy, the Taylor family back in St Louis reckoned that England was doomed, at the very least, to a rapid German invasion, and that relatives should be summoned home with all possible speed. Francis Taylor therefore put his wife and children on a boat bound for New York, with the promise that he would be following just as soon as the gallery could be closed up and the paintings either sold off or shipped back to St Louis.

Sailing out of Southampton on the last crossing of the liner *Manhattan*, Mrs Taylor and her son and daughter were in fact en route for California, since their husband and father had not yet finally decided where in the USA he would now take his branch of the family business. Los Angeles, however, seemed to make considerable sense, in that most of Mrs Taylor's family was now living there and the Hollywood movie community was already ensuring a rich collection of art lovers or at any rate art purchasers. Moreover, some of the artists Taylor had met and represented in London, including Augustus John, were looking for American representation, and the idea of an upmarket gallery, situated perhaps in a good hotel lobby and specializing in European art, seemed an unusually good one to all the Taylor relatives back home.

On board the *Manhattan*, Mrs Taylor took Elizabeth to see her first film, a Shirley Temple musical which seems to have done nothing to deter the other child's eagerness to act; the idea of a showbiz *Gypsy* mother eagerly pushing her daughter toward the already waiting California cameras is, however, one that Mrs Taylor herself has always been at some pains to deny: 'Just because I had once been an actress myself, people always took it for granted that I had ambitions for my child. Nothing could be further from the truth: first of all, we never needed the money, and secondly I not only gave up the theatre when I married, I also never regretted my decision in all the years afterwards. What I really wanted for Elizabeth was that she should get back to school in England and to the riding she so loved there, but the war now made that impossible.'

It is still possible to find casting agents and even producers in the Hollywood hills who take a rather different view, recalling Mrs Taylor's eagerness to get her only daughter in front of the cameras; but that certainly was not yet an ambition of her husband's. Francis Taylor had demanded that Sara should abandon acting on her marriage, and he certainly was not now about to have any child of his start up the greasepaint tradition again. Not that he was in much danger of that from his son: on the one occasion when it was mooted that Howard might like to take a camera test, the boy instantly shaved his head to counter the threat of an acting career.

Accordingly, the family took up residence in Pasadena and Francis Taylor opened his hotel-lobby art gallery at the Château Elysée, though he was soon able to move to a richer if no more chic clientele at the Beverly Hills Hotel. Already the Taylors were therefore surrounded by movie people and movie gossip: the talk of the year was *Gone With The Wind*, and more than one mother at Hawthorne School in Beverly Hills told Mrs Taylor that as her daughter looked remarkably like Vivien Leigh, and could even sound English, the sooner she was tested for Scarlett O'Hara's daughter in the movie the better. Mrs Taylor let that one go by, however, and it was not until early in 1941, by which time Elizabeth was rising nine and had been back in California almost two years, that the subject of an acting career came up again.

This time it was a visitor to Francis Taylor's art gallery, Andrea Chowdin, who saw 'the most beautiful child I have ever seen: she didn't walk, she danced, and she had a lovely singing voice too . . . at that time you didn't know what she'd be, but you knew she'd be something.'

Mrs Chowdin just happened to be married to the chairman of the board at Universal, and it was there that Elizabeth was soon taken by her mother for an audition: any parental opposition still evident from her father seemed to be disappearing because, as her mother noted, 'Elizabeth just seemed to want to do it so badly.' Universal in those days was still a small family studio, and the Taylors regarded it as a safe home for their young daughter, much safer in fact that MGM, which was where Elizabeth really wanted to be as it was a lot closer to home, the family having now forsaken Pasadena for an address in Hollywood itself. But although Metro, hearing of Universal's interest in 'the new girl', were offering a seven-year contract at a hundred dollars a week on the strength of one studio scout having seen her at dance class, Universal confirmed their lead by offering two hundred dollars a week and a contract which could be more easily broken if either side felt that it had been a mistake.

Which it was. Uncertain what to do with their expensive new nine-year-old, and denied the vast riches of the MGM script department, Universal threw Taylor into an hour-long B-to-Z comedy of breathtaking awfulness which required her to support a child star by the name of Alfalfa from the *Our Gang* successes. Thus it was that the actress who twenty years later was to take more money out of movies than any other made her screen début in *Man or Mouse*, a title which seemed so awful even to those who had actually made the movie that they rapidly changed it on release to *There's One Born Every Minute*. All Miss Taylor could later recall was that 'I had to run around a lot and shoot rubber bands at ladies' bottoms', and the film was mercifully not long enough to get formally reviewed. Carl Switzer, the child star known as Alfalfa, died in a gun battle in 1959, the year that his co-star in *Man or Mouse* made her first million dollars from *Cleopatra*.

For now, however, Universal had a problem. The child to whom they were paying an unusually high two hundred dollars a week was patently not turning out to be the next Deanna Durbin, let alone the next Shirley Temple, and at ten she was soon going to be over the hill for lovable moppets. The studio's own casting department now took

The first film: a 1942 low-budget comedy called *There's One Born Every Minute* in which Taylor dimly recalls playing 'a beastly child' opposite Carl 'Alfalfa' Switzer of the *Our Gang* series.

the view that they had made a ghastly mistake: 'Taylor's eyes are too old', read a memo in late 1941, 'and she doesn't even have the face of a kid.' It was agreed on all sides that the contract would be allowed to drop as soon as possible. Elizabeth went back to the Hawthorne School a little sadder and wiser maybe, but at least able to answer the endless questions about why she was not going to be an actress with the news that she had tried it and failed.

And had it not been for Pearl Harbor, that might well have been that. The Taylors were after all not studio people, and Elizabeth (although English by a geographical accident of birth) had settled back into her American heritage which meant that she in no way belonged to that California Raj of expatriate British gentlemen actors who were still making most of the classic movies at Metro. She was patently not a child star in the Temple/Durbin mould, nor was she a compulsive entertainer like the young Judy Garland, or a definably Hollywood child like Natalie Wood. Taylor was just a good-looking little girl who happened to be growing up in Beverly Hills on her way perhaps to a rich marriage . . . to someone like Nicky Hilton of the hotel chain, maybe. There was no particular reason why she had to do any commercial acting along the path to what was still the all-American domestic dream.

What changed all that, albeit accidentally, was the attack on Pearl Harbor in December 1941. Besides bringing America into the war, the Japanese air force managed to convince hundreds of Californians that a full-scale invasion of the Hollywood beaches was only a matter of days away. Leading figures of the Los Angeles community, among them studio executives and art dealers, were co-opted almost immediately for a variety of semimilitary duties including those of air raid wardens. The fact that no Japanese aircraft had been sighted flying low over MGM was not considered conclusive proof of Californian aerial safety, and thus it was that early in 1942 the studio executive Sam Marx would frequently find himself on sky-scanning duty alongside temporary acting Air Raid Warden Francis Taylor.

In the absence of any Japanese pouring out of the night skies, Mr Marx and Mr Taylor would also find themselves of an evening discussing their respective families, and it was therefore not long before Mr Marx discovered that Mr Taylor had a daughter of just ten who despite an early fiasco at Universal still quite liked the idea of becoming an actress. Nor was it long before Mr Taylor discovered that Mr Marx had a picture on the MGM lot in a certain amount of trouble: admittedly it was a B picture, and starring a new dog called Lassie at that, but the trouble was to do with the little girl cast as the daughter of the Duke who owned the dog. The talent of Maria Flynn was not in question: she had, however, suddenly grown too tall for the child star of the picture, Roddy McDowall, and would have to be replaced with the film already in front of the cameras.

Whether you believe the theory that the Taylor parents were still none too keen to have their girl in movies, and were therefore merely doing Mr Marx a favour in his hour of casting need, or whether you believe that they were in fact desperate to give Elizabeth another studio chance and that Mr Marx was therefore doing them a favour, doesn't in the long run matter any more than Bogart's proverbial hill of beans. What happened was that MGM in mid-audition for a *Lassie* girl replacement suddenly happened upon a ten-year-old who, having spent seven of her years in England, could not only sound like the daughter of Nigel Bruce she was supposed in the movie to be, but could also ride a horse as to the English saddle born.

Talent was not an issue here. Taylor looked right, sounded right and rode right for the role of Priscilla, and within days it was hers. Not, admittedly, that it was a star part; this belonged to Lassie (in fact a male dog called Pal who was rumoured to have served with distinction in the German Army), while the human players included a starry roster of the Hollywood British: not only McDowall and 'Willy' Bruce, the definitive Dr Watson in the *Sherlock Holmes* movies with Basil Rathbone, but also Alan Napier, Edmund Gwenn, Donald Crisp, Dame May Whitty, Ben Webster and Mrs Charles Laughton (Elsa Lanchester). Up against a group like that, Taylor didn't have much hope of critical recognition, though *Variety* did note the arrival on screen of 'a pretty moppet who shows up to good advantage'.

But *Lassie Come Home* was as good a way as any of starting a Hollywood career, even if you weren't canine. The film led to seven sequels and a television serial that ran nineteen years, it got Taylor's violet eyes into Technicolor for the first time; and it established her at Metro as a useful, hard-working little girl, well worth the year's contract they were now prepared to offer while they thought about what else she might be able to do.

For Elizabeth herself the film meant an introduction to her lifelong friend and ally Roddy McDowall, to the studio where she would remain under contract for the next seventeen years, and to the life that she now decided she most wanted to lead in front of the cameras – not because of any burning desire or dedication to acting, but simply because it seemed like more fun than anything else she could have been doing at the time. On that simple and straightforward basis, Miss Taylor was to run a career of fifty movies and a life of seven marriages: we are not here dealing with an actress who became a star, but rather with a child star who became an actress in later life.

The 'kid who had nothing' in the eyes of the Universal

casting department now had an MGM contract, one which allowed her to be immediately loaned out to Fox for *Jane Eyre*, though in a role so far down the cast-list (one of Jane's schoolgirl friends in a flashback) that she was virtually unbilled. Indeed she was appalled to find, when she gathered one of her subsequent families around a television set to watch it years later, that her sequence had been entirely cut from the print. This was the Orson Welles/Joan Fontaine version (in fact the fifth on screen, though only the second with dialogue), and as early as 1945 Bosley Crowther had noted that the school sequence involving Taylor seemed 'remote from the rest of the picture, indeed almost a separate tale'.

Nevertheless it was a fine film to have been seen in, if only fleetingly, and Taylor did have one good brief scene as an orphan dying of pneumonia: she was again working with several of the Hollywood English, and when MGM took her back into the fold it was for yet another of the Raj pictures and this time one of the best. *The White Cliffs of Dover* belonged to that group of 'mythical British' Hollywood movies in which an Englishman's home was always his castle, preferably gothic, where the upper classes kept dogs and stiff upper lips while the lower orders were either reverent old retainers or music-hall turns. This one in fact derived from a patriotic poem by Alice Duer Miller, and essentially concerned Irene Dunne getting widowed in the First World War and living to see her son wounded in the Second World War. Taylor was again cast opposite Roddy

McDowall, in what was now becoming one of the more popular double-acts on the Metro set.

True, they weren't exactly Judy Garland and Mickey Rooney, but at the height of these British Empire sagas they were about the only kids around who could pass for English, even if their clenched good manners were now in some danger of disappearing into their Californian tans. Children who had lived by the pools of Beverly Hills since 1939 did not admittedly bear much resemblance to those who were living through a European war, but then Hollywood's England was never meant to be a real England either: instead it was a never-never land of screenwriters' imagination, wrapped all year round in dense fog, a land where people lived usually in castles and were much addicted to fox-hunting at the height of summer, except for Sir C. Aubrey Smith who usually sat as a Duke in the House of Commons while cheerful cockney barrow-boys danced on the surrounding pavements.

Of this endearing if increasingly unreal world, Taylor was now becoming the Crown Princess: a London childhood, and an increasingly wealthy Californian art dealer father, together with a mother who carefully emphasized her daughter's Englishness whenever possible, gave Taylor a useful edge over the other studio children of her generation. Not only did she photograph well ('not make-up but me' she sharply told a director who once complained of too much mascara and eyebrow pencil), and have an accurate memory for the vowel sounds of Hampstead and Kent, but she also had patently not been dragged up on the wrong side of American tracks by parents desperate to make some money out of her ringlets. At a time when *Mrs Miniver* was the biggest moneymaker around, and MGM's senior serving officers and ladies and gentlemen were still people like Aubrey Smith and May Whitty and Gladys Cooper (all of whom were with Taylor in *White Cliffs*), Liz at eleven was about the only little girl on the lot who could instantly join their family.

But three very small roles in big pictures and one starry start in a Universal disaster did not amount to a spectacular two years in Hollywood studios, and though she now had the relative security of an MGM contract for her daughter, Mrs Taylor was in no doubt that she had to go up for the big one. Five years earlier, the role of Scarlett O'Hara in *Gone With The Wind* had been the ambition of just about every actress under sixty on every studio lot; but there was another project which had been around even longer and was still the ambition of just about every actress under twenty.

In 1935 the English novelist and dramatist Enid Bagnold had published a major bestseller about a butcher's daughter in Sussex who wins a horse in a raffle and goes on to win the Grand National, in which she rides it disguised as a boy. For nearly a decade, Pandro Berman had been trying to cast the movie. His first idea, Katharine Hepburn, was now well into her thirties and thus somewhat over the hill for the transvestite jockey. Other possible casting had included Margaret Sullavan and Margaret O'Brien and, most intriguingly, another London evacuee by the name of Shirley Catlin, who was to achieve in later life an altogether different kind of fame as the Social Democrat leader Shirley Williams.

But the problem with such well-publicized talent hunts for a specific role was that in the end everyone lost interest in the film itself. The right Velvet just didn't seem to be around, so the project was indefinitely shelved until MGM's story department noted that it had another and hitherto unexpected asset. The script also featured a star role for an actor small enough to play the disillusioned jockey who gets Velvet and her horse over the hurdles, and Mickey Rooney had to be found a big film for 1944. Thus the endless search for the 'right' Velvet became incidental: the film had to be made for Rooney anyway, and the studio would go with the most likely girl around.

Taylor had kept her riding and her English accent in trim for just such an opportunity, and MGM now realized what they had got in her: the yearly contract immediately became a seven-year deal with few options, and Mrs Taylor was now taken on to the studio payroll as her daughter's official minder. Publicity handouts revealed how determinedly Taylor had 'grown' for the role (not altogether difficult when you consider Rooney's diminutive stature) and how courageously she had behaved in the face of temperamental horses on a previous picture, *Lassie Come Home*, when one had stepped on her toe and caused it to swell to such an extent that the boot had to be cut off around it.

There was at this time a curiously obsessive desire by Metro and the Taylor family to suggest to the public that Elizabeth and horses had some sort of near-mystical connection, but when *National Velvet* eventually opened in London, at least one critic (the revered Campbell Dixon of the *Daily Telegraph*) reckoned the whole relationship was thoroughly unhealthy: 'The child is a pathological case. Whenever she speaks or thinks about horses – and that is all the time, since she even practises horsemanship in bed – her strange, sooty eyes gleam and her whole frame trembles with the intensity of her passion. Whether this is healthy in a small girl or even a big girl is a problem I leave to parents, psychiatrists and horse-lovers without confidence of unanimity.'

But *National Velvet* was certainly healthy at the box-office: 'the top click of the year' there according to *Variety*; and the picture achieved a sell-out run at Radio City music hall in New York over the Christmas of 1944. A grateful studio, recognizing early in the shooting that this was to be Elizabeth Taylor's rather than Rooney's picture, duly gave her a gold star on the dressing-room door – and indeed the horse on which she rode to stardom in the National, this last a somewhat dubious gift since it turned out to be extremely lame and was to live on in long retirement at Taylor's expense.

With Mickey Rooney in the film that made her a star: *National Velvet* (1944).

30

Engaged to be Engaged

'From the very beginning, I began to see myself as two quite separate people: Elizabeth Taylor the person and Elizabeth Taylor the studio commodity. But I was a person before I was in films, and whatever the public thought of me I knew who I was'

National Velvet had made Taylor at twelve the star she was to remain for the next forty years, and hers was always to be a curiously Olympic kind of stardom. Like the female jockey she played here, she had literally hurdled her way to success, and the career which followed was always to resemble a Grand National obstacle course rather than a coherent attempt to make a living out of being an actress. Her father was in later life to note rather sadly that this was the film where he lost a daughter and a wife: its immense success meant that both the women in his family now devoted themselves single-mindedly to Elizabeth Taylor enterprises to such an extent that horse-brasses were soon to be found all over his living-room.

The Taylor brand of stardom was something new to the industry as well as the family. Where earlier moppets like Shirley Temple and Deanna Durbin, and indeed Rooney and Garland, had made it by being lovable or musical or preferably both, Taylor offered an altogether more distant image, a little girl in love with her horse (*National Velvet*) or her dog (*Lassie*) and only reluctantly prepared to let the audience into her private world of child-animal alliance. This was something altogether different, and American audiences responded to it with considerable fervour; indeed Taylor's memory of the night the war ended in Europe was of being mobbed on a railway station in Chicago while changing trains on a promotional tour.

There were other biographical elements which also suggested that Taylor was to be the first in a new post-war breed of studio stars. Nowhere in her life had there been the ritual economic or professional struggle that was historically supposed to lead to the bright lights, nor had she been traditionally discovered by a casting agent. In an almost regal way, she had just been there when she was needed and answered the call. Her relationship with the studio where she was in fact to stay from *National Velvet* all the way through to *Cleopatra* at the end of the 1950s was therefore not one of gratitude or delight or amazement or respect for the old moguls. MGM was just the factory where they made her films, and if anything separated Taylor from the pre-war stars of the Joan Crawford/Bette Davis era, it was perhaps this early recognition of the cinema as an industry rather than a calling.

For 1945 and a perspicacious if lonely child, this was an intelligent foresight of the new Hollywood, and Elizabeth was the first of its more distanced and independent industrial creations, an employee of the studio with certain voting rights in her own destiny rather than yet another unquestioning niece of old uncle Louis B. Mayer. The art of movies had already become a business, and so far from the wide-eyed theatrical Kate Hepburn of *Stage Door*, the role model now for the Taylors (mother and daughter) was more likely to have been Rosalind Russell, storming hitherto all-male boardrooms in a sharp suit with a sharper line of expenses.

Officially, however, Liz remained a studio schoolgirl, albeit one now given top billing for the film which followed *National Velvet*: this was *The Courage of Lassie*, since Metro and their audiences had now decided that their little girl was, like Doctor Dolittle, at her best when talking to the animals or at any rate nuzzling her auburn locks against their necks. This new *Lassie* achieved some sort of record by not showing a human on screen for all of its first twenty minutes, but there was still a certain amount of confusion about the dog of the title. All through the dialogue Taylor refers to her beloved collie as 'Bill', while the film itself was made under the alternative titles *Blue Sierra* and *Hold High the Torch*. Nobody seems to have mentioned or even thought of Lassie in this context

'Growing up in Hollywood never struck me as the glamorous existence you read about in magazines' *Elizabeth Taylor*; 'Taylor is refreshingly natural as Lassie's devoted owner.' *New York Times*

WISH DEEPLY FOR *THY* WEAL
WISH DEEPLY AND THY WISH CONCEAL
ONE THING MORE THOU NEEDST MUST DO
BELIEVE THY WISH IS COMING TRUE

until the film was virtually on release, whereupon some studio executive belatedly noticed the absurd waste in a title about a little girl and a big dog going out to the nation's cinemas with no reference to the one name guaranteed to form queues for this kind of entertainment.

Accordingly it was rapidly retitled, even though no dog answers to the name of Lassie anywhere in the picture. Way down the cast-list, billed fifteenth in fact and merely as 'First Youth', was the unfortunate Carl 'Alfalfa' Switzer, who had starred in Taylor's first movie four short years earlier: if she needed any reminder about the danger of putting your fate in the hands of movie moguls, it was already there.

She and her mother therefore weighed into their first great studio battle reasonably well prepared. Though Taylor was later to write of *National Velvet* as 'the most heavenly moment of my working life', that did not mean accepting the notion that Louis B. Mayer was God. True, he or his workers had made her a star, but in return she had given them a marathon box-office winner in *National Velvet* and a couple of money-making *Lassies* into the bargain. So it was not as a supplicant that she (and her mother) approached the studio boss with a request that she be allowed to film *Sally*, a script which would allow her to sing and dance and generally get away from horses and dogs for a while. Mayer seems to have taken their request as an unwarrantable invasion of his right to decide what his contract artists should do next. He and Mrs Taylor therefore had, in front of the teenage Liz, a blazing and linguistically colourful row, with Mayer going into his usual routine about having raised a star from the gutter, only to be sharply reminded by Mrs Taylor that he was dealing with a family of distinguished art dealers and not his usual Californian rubbish. The row ended with Mayer telling Mrs Taylor she was so goddamned stupid she couldn't spot the day of the week, whereupon Elizabeth told him never again to dare to speak to her mother like that. Both women then stormed out of his office and Liz swore that she would never again visit Mayer, a resolution she remarkably managed to keep for the five more years that he remained as head of her studio. On the other hand, she never got to film *Sally*.

Nevertheless, she was now at fifteen on $750 a week, plus a $15,000 bonus for *National Velvet*'s worldwide success, and moreover a studio child at Metro in an era when her fellow studio contract players included Judy Garland, Spencer Tracy, Lana Turner, Hedy Lamarr and Clark Gable. Metro's all-powerful press office was also keen to capitalize on the fact that she looked and photographed vastly older than her years, so that the 'pretty moppet' spotted by *Variety* in *Lassie Come Home* was only two years later getting her first screen kiss from Jimmy Lydon in an otherwise forgettable film version of a Broadway flop about the social and sexual awakening of an invalid teenager and known variously as *Cynthia* or *The Rich Full Life*.

The story of Elizabeth Taylor has always been the history of marketing movies rather than their art, and it started as early as this: to coincide with the first release of *Cynthia*, cinemas across America were inspired by MGM to run contests entitled 'Why I Deserve to be Kissed by Liz' – winners to receive not the actual kiss but a couple of free tickets to the movie. At the same time, the studio released her first published work, *Nibbles and Me*, a glutinous schoolgirl essay about life with a pet chipmunk which nevertheless sold several thousand copies, principally to middle-aged matrons who saw in Taylor the kind of clean-cut, animal-loving teenage daughter they would most like to have had themselves.

At an immediately post-war moment, when real-life teenagers were already starting to rebel, Taylor's great on-screen attractions were stability and maturity. Her image was not that of the saccharine Shirley Temple or Deanna Durbin, nor yet of the more dangerous and unstable Judy Garland. Instead she offered a distant, withdrawn, aristocratic girl who was still happiest talking to the animals but who knew her place as a kind of mythical Miss Miniver. 'Her face,' wrote Bosley Crowther in the *New York Times*, 'is alive with youthful spirit, her voice has the softness of sweet song and her whole manner is of refreshing grace.' In short she had come from the other side of the Atlantic, and therefore knew a thing or two about style and grace and refinement at a time when those qualities were not much in evidence among Ameri-

With James
Lydon from
whom she
received her
first screen kiss
in *Cynthia*
(1947).

can teenagers on screen or off. Even the normally more acerbic James Agee was bowled over: 'Ever since I first saw this child, I have been choked with the peculiar sort of adoration I might have felt if we were in the same grade of primary school.'

Taylor's studio publicists also knew a thing or two about how to handle the nationality issue. Her Englishness was useful up to a point, in that it gave her an edge over the other teenage studio children, but even at this early stage she had to take care not to seem in any way anti-American. In a carefully planted interview with Hedda Hopper early in 1947, Taylor accordingly revealed: 'I love England and I want to visit there and make pictures, but America is where my parents were born and where my friends are and where my work is and I feel that I am an American now. I shall be very proud on the day I take the oath of allegiance.'

By now, despite the quarrel with Mayer, MGM had taken over Taylor's life to the point where she was being educated between takes at the little red schoolhouse on the studio backlot, and though her mother was still much in evidence as the personal manager of her daughter's career, both her father and her brother seemed to have resigned themselves to losing her from the home life of the family. From here until 1960, only one year would go by without the release of at least one Taylor movie, and in these late 1940s and early 1950s the annual total would more usually rise to three or even four. She was now a creature of the Metro studio machine at its most prolific and powerful, and though off-camera she herself always maintained a jokily cynical view of the problems of being a studio child ('It is not easy,' she once noted, 'to get a thorough education when Robert Taylor keeps sticking his tongue down your throat'), on camera she cheerfully did whatever a succession of contract directors and producers thought most likely to keep a queue of the faithful forming at box-offices around the nation and indeed the world.

There was, however, a certain confusion here: having risen to fame rapidly in a quintessentially little-girl sequence of the two *Lassies* and *National Velvet*, Taylor had ceased to be a little girl vastly more rapidly than the likes of Deanna Durbin or even Judy Garland. Her bust, like that of Mrs Worthington's daughter, was rather too developed for her age, and that physical asset together with a distinctly unchildlike manner on screen meant that her career as a little girl was as short-lived on camera as off. 1947, her sixteenth year, was the one in which MGM lent her out to Warner's for *Life With Father*, a Broadway long-runner of over three thousand performances which told of the upstairs-downstairs life of an 1880s New York household. Taylor was billed third to William Powell and Irene Dunne and managed to display a puppy-love infatuation for her new screen boyfriend Jimmy Lydon, but this was already the end of the period in which she was expected to play roles devoid of real sexuality.

For the first but by no means last time, she interrupted the shooting schedule here for reasons of shaky health: five studio days were lost (and her paypacket accordingly adjusted) at just about the moment when it was being strongly rumoured that Mrs Taylor had started an affair

with the film's director, Michael Curtiz, thereby
somewhat disrupting home life with mother.

But as soon as *Life With Father* was completed on the
Warner lot, Elizabeth returned to the arms of MGM for
Cynthia, the film that gave her top billing and a title role
as well as the chance to grow up on camera. Mary Astor,
playing her mother in this, noted a cool and rather
superior teenager, lacking Garland's warmth but pos-
sessed of a calculating determination to succeed which
was doubtless more useful around a studio as crowded as
Metro with potential rivals. One of them, Jane Powell, was
the star of Taylor's next picture. This was *A Date with
Judy*, a rare and dire musical based on a radio series of the
time and featuring the band of Xavier Cugat – though not
a lot else, unless you count Wallace Beery being taught to
rumba by Carmen Miranda – in a plot of mind-boggling
inanity through which Taylor moved with her customary
air of elegant distaste.

But *A Date with Judy* did no lasting harm to Taylor's
career: indeed *Variety* thought her beauty 'breathtaking',
while Otis Guernsey for the *New York Herald Tribune*
went a lot further: 'The erstwhile child star of *National
Velvet* has been touched by Metro's magic wand and
turned into a real 14-carat 100-proof siren with a whole
new career opening in front of her . . . Hedy Lamarr had
better watch out.' Tactfully, nobody referred to the fact
that her one song in the picture had to have its high notes
sung by an entirely different lady.

In the light of her now-considerable popularity, and the fact that her mother was still a formidable contract negotiator, MGM put Taylor's salary up to a thousand dollars a week for 1948, more than any other contract artist of her generation was making at the time and also more than most of the other adult members of the Hollywood Raj of English expatriates were making. Not that Taylor ever belonged in those ranks; and although local papers at home would still describe her as 'English-born', the accent no longer bore many traces of Golders Green, and it was not entirely easy to lead the life of an average London teenager when under the Hollywood arc lights at two hundred dollars a day.

1948 was also the year in which she started out on a love life of considerable complication: she fell first for Peter Lawford, with whom she was partnered in *Julia Misbehaves*, a curious screen adaptation of the old Margery Sharp bestseller designed to establish Greer Garson as a classy screwball comedienne in the tradition of Carole Lombard. As Miss Garson was nothing of the kind, but a matronly and rather humourless figure from the wartime Raj heyday of *Mrs Miniver*, the film unsurprisingly fell very flat at the box-office. It did, however, bring Taylor into an embrace with Lawford, the intensity of which disturbed several onlookers, not least Mrs Taylor and studio publicists, uneasily aware that their girl had only just celebrated her sixteenth birthday, despite the fact that their make-up department had her looking about twenty-five. Clearly an affair with Lawford, ten years her senior, was not something to be encouraged even if they had started out together in *The White Cliffs of Dover* and were now going on to *Little Women*. On the other hand someone vaguely suitable had to be found to escort a valuable property to Metro's frequent premieres around Hollywood, and the rather less raffish Marshall Thompson was thus pressed into service as Taylor's first official boyfriend.

That did not last long, however, and she was soon in open rebellion against her many career advisers: 'The people in the MGM press department would suggest that I date somebody, but nobody was going to tell me whom to date or what to wear.' The curious thing about Taylor at

this time, and what separated her from most of her studio contemporaries, was an almost total lack of ambition. Unlike most of them, she had not come up the hard way through a background of poverty or parental deprivation or family disasters: she had not had to sit around the bar stools of drugstores awaiting discovery, nor serve any kind of theatrical apprenticeship. Totally protected by mother and the studio, she simply glided from movie to movie without apparent effort. Because it was the only life she had ever really known, it never occurred to her to wonder whether she could really do it or not. Spared therefore the agonies of insecurity or script choice, since that too was handled by the studio, her only real worry was a rapidly increasing boredom factor. Escape from the studios now became a primary objective: escape into the Hollywood hills, where she would ride her beloved horses; escape into movie theatres, where she could watch films without actively having to make them; escape into a daydream of early marriage to someone who would take her away from the need to make another couple of dramas by Christmas. Taylor seldom went into open rebellion against her Hollywood employers, since that too went against the grain of a well-brought-up young English-

With Marshall Thompson, an early escort, at the premiere of *The Yearling*; and back on the National-winner as Velvet.

woman: but MGM can seldom have had on their studio register a contract artist who found those studios quite so oppressively tedious. Even Lassie displayed more enthusiasm for the scripts.

It soon began to occur to Liz that the perfect escape would be an early marriage: ever a romantic, brought up on a diet of the teenage fiction she was usually filming as well as reading between shots, she announced to an early interviewer that she was 'an emotional child inside a woman's body' and that she could never have an affair, only a marriage – a policy to which she adhered rigorously through seven marriages across forty years.

Finding a prospective fiancé did not prove too difficult: the first rule was to avoid any actor, since that would mean more studios and the continuing lack of any non-cinematic life. Happily one Sunday, a Metro publicist took her to a Malibu party where another guest was Glenn Davis, a clean-cut all-American army football hero who subsequently presented her with a diamond ring in return for an announcement via Hedda Hopper that the couple were 'engaged to be engaged'.

With Peter Lawford in *Little Women* (1949); and with Glenn Davis, her first fiancé, a few months earlier.

Taylor herself was later to dismiss the romance as 'childish', but she did keep the gossips happy by wearing Davis's gold football around her neck. In many ways he was perfect casting, a former co-captain of the West Point team who had gone on to star as captain of both basket-

ball and baseball teams before embarking on a chaste but promising alliance with Elizabeth. Meanwhile her apparent lack of enthusiasm for the actual making of movies was causing considerable distress, not least to her still starstruck mother. It wasn't that she was any real trouble on the set, though she had already perfected a lifelong technique of only doing any acting when the cameras were actually rolling, thereby rendering any rehearsals both unnecessary and uneventful. But she had made it very clear there were other places she would rather be, thereby provoking an indignant enquiry from her mother about whether she was now planning altogether to abandon a promising career.

On balance, Taylor decided she was not: to the relief of Sara, still on a studio retainer of several thousand dollars a year as her daughter's offcial minder, Liz wrote in a note of filial apology, 'I realize that my whole life has been in motion pictures and for me to quit now would be like cutting away the roots of a tree . . . I've made up my mind for myself, so I'll take all the hardships and everything else that comes along because I know (and I'll always realize) that I was the one who chose to stay in and that I'm the one who must take them without grumbling or wanting to quit.'

So in she stayed, going next into a remake of *Little Women* (in fact the third and last version of Louisa May Alcott's sugary classic, unless you count a fourth with Shirley Temple and Jennifer Jones which was mysteriously closed down after three weeks of shooting) as the selfish, conceited Amy, a role which at least allowed her to wear a blonde wig and pursue her on-screen infatuation with Peter Lawford. But the film itself was a pale replica of the George Cukor/Katharine Hepburn masterpiece from 1933, and the most that could really be said for Taylor in it was that she managed to distance herself a little from the saccharine sweetness of Janet Leigh, Margaret O'Brien and June Allyson as the rest of the sorority.

Meanwhile the 'engagement' to Glenn Davis was already running aground: in the autumn of 1948 the 24-year-old lieutenant was shipped out to a tour of duty in Korea for six months, thereby giving Taylor time to reflect

At seventeen, back home in London for her first English shooting on *Conspirator* (1949).

that though the press, gently encouraged by MGM's publicity machine, thought of it as what Liz called 'a big hot romance', this was in fact nothing of the kind. That realization fully dawned on her during a rare return to London, whither MGM sent her and Robert Taylor to make what they billed as 'Elizabeth Taylor's First Adult Love Story'. This turned out to be a catastrophic Cold War drama called *The Conspirator*, written in the first flush of Hollywood's anti-Communist panic but so shakily that even with the suitably red-baiting script, the studio held up its release for fully thirteen months while they wondered whether its patriotic conclusion could possibly overcome its general awfulness.

The answer to that was in the negative: 'a lugubrious affair', thought the *New York Times*, and Taylor was indeed not at her best trying to express the anguish of a young wife who discovers that her husband is a Soviet spy. The most savage attack came from the *Harvard*

Lampoon, a college newspaper which gave Liz its annual award for 'so gallantly persisting in her career despite an inability to act' and named her the year's 'most objectionable ingénue'. At seventeen that cannot have been the most encouraging of notices; but Taylor already had twelve films in the can, not to mention a supportive studio and a mother still fervently promoting her daughter's career on both sides of the Atlantic. Against a defence system such as that, there was little that even Harvard could manage beyond the occasional jeer from the sidelines.

The trip to London, and a brief visit from there to Paris, had however alerted Elizabeth to the fact that even in a post-war depression there was still a life in Europe, one rather more intriguing and sophisticated than could be found on the beaches or sound stages of California. Once she was back there, the all-American romance with Glenn Davis lurched to an abrupt halt and she became almost immediately engaged instead to William D. Pawley, an infinitely wealthier son of a former American ambassador to Brazil. Pawley was a more cosmopolitan figure than Davis, a founder of the Miami Bachelors Club and a man who since then had travelled the world before returning to Florida to make a fortune of his own. At twenty-eight he was fully a decade older than Taylor and keen for her to abandon a studio contract that was now making a thousand dollars a week for his future bride.

What Pawley was offering, beyond a three-and-a-half carat diamond engagement ring (the second of nearly a dozen that she was to collect along the way to her half-century) was exactly what Elizabeth now seemed most to want and to fear: an escape from the clutches of Metro and her mother, but also an end to any thoughts of an acting career; as she retired into a world that would be no less wealthy or glamorous than the one she was giving up for him. Pawley was therefore to become the new man in her young life, and she duly got engaged to him, just as in the future she would duly get engaged and married to every man with whom she ever fell, however transiently, in love. In there somewhere, but seldom visible to her critics in the popular press, was a strict if eccentric kind of serial monogamy: all affairs had to be formalized almost at

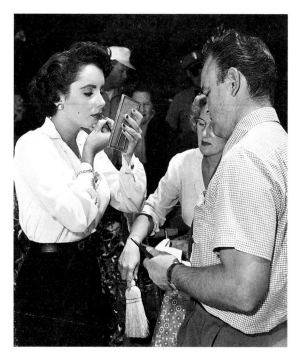

With Van
Johnson in *The
Big Hangover*
(1949); and in
*Father of the
Bride*, father
this time being
Spencer Tracy.

once, even if the formalization then had to be unscrambled again a year or two later.

And so it was with Pawley: he seemed a better bet than Glenn Davis, both financially and in his classier social background, and marriage to him would probably be close enough to the kind of marriage she might have made back in England to a scion of one of the better country houses that were still a part of her mother's fond memories and maternal ambitions. Taylor herself, however, was not so sure, as she later noted: 'I wore Bill's ring for a few months . . . we went well together under the palm trees, we looked nice on the dance floor, we loved to go boating. But we had nothing in common in our lives.'

The real problem here was work: for all her restiveness at Metro, Taylor had a contract to fulfil, and although this could still throw her into such horrors as *Conspirator* and the one with which she followed it, an altogether mindless and witless romantic comedy called *The Big Hangover* in which she was helped by neither Van Johnson nor a talking dog in other leading roles, there were signs at last that one or two studio executives had begun to realize they now had something more than just another leftover child star on their payroll. Even Elizabeth, though she was already talking to the ever-sentimental Hedda Hopper of honeymoon cottages with roses around the door, seemed

46

aware that she could hardly end her career with the run of movies she had recently been making.

What brought that career back from an early grave was the first good script she'd read since *Life With Father*. This one, too, was built around Metro's devotion to family sagas involving powerful father-figures not unlike Louis B. Mayer and headstrong daughters not unlike Taylor herself. *Father of the Bride* was a film distinguished by Spencer Tracy's infinitely weary, wry performance as the bemused and embattled father losing a daughter only to gain the vast expense of her wedding. With Vincente Minnelli directing, and a supporting cast which featured Joan Bennett as the constantly shopping mother and Russ Tamblyn as the little brother, this was a sketchy but amiably cynical account of the mechanics and economics of a small-town American marriage, and it seems to have given Taylor a taste for the ceremony at least, since she was to go through four of them before the next decade was out.

It also seems to have revived her interest in films and filming, and ironically therefore, in view of its subject, proved to be the unmaking of her plans to marry Pawley. What he expected, as a pre-condition of their life together, was her immediate and total retirement from the screen and a move to the family home-state of Florida, there to settle into the blissful domesticity that Taylor had by now told all available journalists was her ultimate dream. That might have happened, had not a better scenario come along. While she was filming *Father of the Bride*, George Stevens at Paramount asked if Elizabeth could be loaned out to them for *A Place in the Sun*, the film he was planning to make from Theodore Dreiser's classic *An American Tragedy*. MGM, still uncertain quite how to treat their now grown-up daughter, were keen enough to recoup some of the costs of her contract, especially as *Father of the Bride* had not yet been released and, with *Conspirator* still on the shelf, she was not at the time proving to be their greatest asset. Taylor, once she had read the screenplay, also realized that she had to do it; the only opposition came from Pawley, who noted that he had already waited for her to finish her last film and that she would now have to choose between him and her next.

Miss Rich Bitch

'For *A Place in the Sun* Elizabeth Taylor and Montgomery Clift are at the top of their careers in the second edition of Dreiser's monumental novel, now a film of beauty, tenderness, power and insight' *New York Times*

*W*ithout too much difficulty, Taylor chose the film. Pawley did the gentlemanly thing, announcing to an aghast Hedda Hopper: 'I love her very much and I believe she loves me, but due to her constant work which all her energy should go into, I feel the only fair thing is to release her from our engagement.' Hedda herself, unusually, refrained from comment, but the rest of the press now began a campaign of moral outrage which was to last through the next thirty years and prove as apparently inexhaustible to its readers as to its writers.

It was a campaign which started in London rather than among the Hollywood gossips of the era: the *Sunday Pictorial*, noting in September 1949 that within the past six months the still seventeen-year-old Taylor had broken off two engagements, announced solemnly that she was 'a living argument against the employment of children in film studios', and added firmly that what she now most needed was a series of 'resounding smacks for being as silly as a schoolboy smoking cigars'. In some curious way, though she had by now been living abroad for almost a decade, the British still regarded Liz as their property, one already somewhat tarnished by nasty foreign habits. As her mother memorably added at this time, 'If I'd known it would turn out like this, I would not have let Elizabeth go into pictures.'

But Taylor was now in pictures, and specifically in one of the best she would ever make. Theodore Dreiser's novel, based on the 1906 murder case concerning the low-born Midwestern youth who killed his pregnant mistress so that he could be free to marry a society girl from the other side of the tracks, had already been filmed once in 1931, and none too successfully, by Josef von Sternberg as a dark psychological thriller, one so loathed by Dreiser that he had tried to have it banned. By the time of the second version twenty years later, he was no longer alive to complain, though apart from its updating to the late 1940s this was to be a reasonably faithful version of the book and one which underlined its broader commentary on the nightmare potential of the upwardly mobile American dream.

A Place in the Sun was a triumph of casting and narrative movie-making. Seeing in Taylor the perfect poor-little-rich-girl characteristics of Angela Vickers, George Stevens had her complete the triangle made up by Montgomery Clift and Shelley Winters, players both of considerably greater adult experience, in what was (as she later remarked) a revelation of screen technique: 'This was the first time I had ever considered *acting* in a film, and it was a tricky part because the girl is so rich and spoiled that it would have been easy to play her as absolutely vacuous. But I think she was a girl who could care a great deal.' Inevitably Liz also managed to fall deeply in love with her co-star, a relationship that was to endure in its own curiously tortured way until Clift died of a heart attack in 1966, considerably the worse for drugs and drink.

At this time, however, he was a hot young property from the New York theatre, already torn between his own homosexuality and a deep love for the blues singer Libby Holman, and unable therefore to deal with Taylor's sudden obsession with him. But he recognized in her a friend who would stand by him from the time of their very first meeting, when Liz was sent by the studio to accompany him to the premiere of his latest success, *The Heiress*, only to have to spend the evening removing his head from his hands at the sight of his own performance.

Stevens was in any case having to rethink his original ideas for the film, since the McCarthy witch-hunt of the

With Clift at the premiere of his *The Heiress*; and together with their director George Stevens on the set of *A Place in the Sun*.

time was making it unfashionable to portray any American social dream of self-improvement as a murderous nightmare. He decided to turn it into a more glossy love story, in which the passion of Taylor for Clift now became the focal point. It photographed well enough, in huge and sexy close-ups of what Stevens called 'the girl on the candy-box cover, the beautiful girl in the yellow Cadillac that every American boy sometime or other thinks he can marry', and it wasn't difficult for Clift, already thoroughly Method-trained by Elia Kazan, to persuade Taylor that he returned her love on screen and even off. Taylor was still an innocent in all sexual matters, and it took her almost the whole length of the shooting to work out that the young men with whom Clift would disappear off the set in the evenings were more than just good friends: 'For days Monty would play the ardent lover with me and we became so close . . . but just as he'd overcome all of his inhibitions about making love he would turn up on the set with some obvious young man that he had picked up and all I could do was sit by helplessly and watch as he threw this in my face.'

Yet despite, or perhaps even because of, that ambiguous off-screen relationship, Taylor and Clift here established a close-up chemistry that is quite remarkable: each seemed to make the other a better and more intense player, and though they were to go through two other screenplays together (the turgid *Raintree County* and then the wonderfully over-the-top *Suddenly Last Summer*) it is in *A Place in the Sun* that they give two of the best performances of their lives, not least because of Stevens's rehearsal trick whereby he would have them play whole scenes in utter silence, working with their eyes and emotions, and only allow them to turn back to the dialogue when the cameras started to roll. If there was a single film that marked Elizabeth's coming-of-age, this was the one. The critic on *Variety* wrote: 'Miss Taylor's histrionics are of a quality so far beyond anything she has done previously that Stevens must be credited with a minor miracle.' Another reviewer noted: 'The conceit, artificiality and awkwardness which marred her playing in ingénue roles are not only acceptable but essential to her rendition here.'

Taylor's playing of Miss Rich Bitch did not put her in line for an Oscar. The film in fact won nine nominations and scooped six actual statues, but none for its players (one of whom, Anne Revere as the mother, saw several of her scenes disappear after being called to testify to the UnAmerican Affairs Committee). And because of Stevens's remarkably slow techniques of editing, not to mention the fact that he had shot several thousand more feet of film than could be used even in a two-hour final cut, *A Place in the Sun* did not get in front of an audience for the next eighteen months, leaving Taylor to return to her Metro contract, having just given the performance of her career, with nothing to show for it beyond the bruises of her passion for Clift.

MGM, unaware that they now had first call on a dramatic actress who had grown out of all recognition in professional stature while working over on the rival Paramount lot, continued only to see Taylor as Spencer Tracy's favourite little girl. The relationship that had worked so well in *Father of the Bride* was thus hauled out of its wedding-day mothballs for a sequel to be called *Father's Little Dividend*, which would feature largely the same cast, once again under Minnelli's direction, and take the story on from the trauma of the marriage to the trauma of the first pregnancy, one handled with an equal amount of soap-operatic sentiment and coy joviality and again really only saved by Tracy's crusty charm.

Faced with what must have seemed like a return to her studio childhood, and still mourning the loss of Clift, who had disappeared back to Libby Holman on the last day of shooting *A Place in the Sun*, Liz was now more than ready for a new romance, and when a chance nightclub encounter brought her face to face with Conrad Nicholas Hilton, son of the chairman of the hotel chain, several prayers seemed to have been simultaneously answered. First of all, he was already vastly wealthier than either of her two previous fiancés, a fact which instantly endeared him to Liz's still watchful parents; secondly, unlike either of his predecessors, he showed no urgent desire for his future wife to abandon her film career unless she actually wanted to do so; thirdly, unlike Clift, he had no very apparent sexual hang-ups; fourthly he even photographed usefully, vaguely resembling the clean-cut all-American youth (Don Taylor) she had recently married on screen in the two Minnelli movies. MGM could scarcely believe their luck: here was a potential marriage made, if not in heaven, then certainly somewhere between the cutting room and the publicity office. If the players could now just get themselves together in reasonably rapid time, it might even be possible to have their wedding coincide with the release of *Father of the Bride*, which was almost ready.

Swept along on this rare tide of adult enthusiasm, Hilton and Taylor, having met in October, were engaged by February and wed by May 1951. True, her father did once express slight reservations about Hilton's playboy past and his demand that Liz should join the Catholic church in order to marry at the right altar, but they were all overcome by Mrs Taylor's enthusiasm for the diamond earrings which came for Christmas and the shares in Hilton Hotels which came soon afterwards. In return for the publicity they would be getting to launch *Father of the Bride*, Metro agreed to finance the entire wedding, and Taylor now took on the roles of bride and Catholic convert as professionally as she had taken on all the others required of her by the studio. Not that the wedding itself went altogether without a hitch: an hour or two beforehand, Bill Pawley turned up on the doorstep of the Taylor home to remind a tearful Liz that she had sworn never to marry anyone else, and during the actual service (better attended, noted one tactless observer, than any other Hollywood ceremony since the Jean Harlow funeral) the organ broke down.

Worse was to follow: the honeymoon couple couldn't get the bridal suite on the *Queen Mary*, as it had already been booked by the long-married Duke and Duchess of Windsor; and Hilton was not best pleased at having to delay the journey abroad so that Liz and Mrs Taylor could as usual celebrate Mother's Day together. By the time he did finally get his bride on to the ship, relations seemed somewhat strained. Though the studio machine had managed to choreograph the wedding, it couldn't do much about the actual marriage, and fellow-passengers noted eagerly some early rifts as Hilton refused to partner his new wife on the dance floor or left their cabin to spend much of the night playing poker.

Hilton's fondness for gambling also proved a problem when they arrived in France, since Liz was still under-age for casinos and had to be left alone again in hotel rooms. When they reached Rome, she relieved her boredom by spending a couple of days as an uncredited extra on the epic *Quo Vadis* that was then being made there; and by the time they got back to California at the end of a long and uneasy summer it was clear even to casual observers, let alone gossip columnists, that something had already gone terribly wrong with the dream marriage of the year.

Hilton himself went through two more unsuccessful marriages before reaching an early grave in 1969 at the age of forty-two, and never commented on his time with Taylor. She also remained silent about it for many years, quite possibly as a condition of the divorce settlement, though after Hilton's death she did occasionally offer scattered clues: 'The honeymoon in Europe lasted two weeks: I should say the marriage lasted for two weeks. Then came disillusionment, rude and brutal.' She had gone into her first marriage at eighteen a sexual innocent,

and was to emerge from it a few months later with ulcers and close to a nervous breakdown. Along the way she had not been much helped by her family or her studio, both of whom begged her to stay with a difficult situation if only to avoid the scandal of a hasty divorce, and it was around now that she began to build up a network of close friends like Roddy McDowall and the errant Montgomery Clift, men who usually posed no sexual hazard but were able to advise her as to her own best interests.

The first of seven weddings: to Nicky Hilton, May 1951.

These clearly pointed toward getting out of the Hilton marriage as soon as possible, and by January 1951 she was in the Santa Monica divorce court. Her parents were still blaming the press for turning 'ordinary honeymoon spats' into something more serious, but Taylor had already moved out of the marital home into an apartment shared with a girlfriend. She herself later recalled, 'When I divorced Nick, I said on the witness stand that he had told me to go to hell and insulted my mother and me in front of friends. They were absolutely the smallest, weakest grounds possible, but they were the only ones I would allow my lawyer to go into.' With a wonderful kind of irony, just as *Father of the Bride* had been perfectly timed to coincide with the wedding, its sequel was released just in time for the divorce.

Determined to establish a separation not only from

Hilton but also from the parents and studio minders with whom she had grown up, and from whom she had derived such total protection that the outside world was only now beginning to become a reality, Taylor began dating a series of men ranging from the billionaire Howard Hughes to the young director Stanley Donen who was to make her next movie. MGM were still in a state of considerable uncertainty about what exactly should be done with her on screen: she had gone almost overnight from fairy-tale princess to nineteen-year-old divorcee, and to make matters worse was now being accused of breaking up a Donen marriage by stealing him from his first wife. This was scarcely what Metro had bargained for in the maturing of their favourite contract daughter; equally, Liz was just beginning to feel that their upbringing had been less than helpful, and that the sooner she established a life and personality of her own, the better it would be for all concerned.

To demonstrate her new-found independence, and well aware that MGM were now paying her the best part of two thousand dollars a week under the original contract which still had over a year to run, she declined to take any alimony from Hilton, though she did decide to keep his wedding gifts, including a Cadillac and the hotel shares;

With her director and good, if self-effacing, friend Stanley Donen at Ciro's.

there was also a property settlement which took several more months to work out. Meanwhile she was seen on the town, not only with Donen and Hughes but a selection of other more or less eligible bachelors and divorcés, all of whom were considered by her parents and her studio minders to be vastly less desirable than the hotel heir she had so recently left.

That, however, was no longer Taylor's concern; what did worry her, and understandably, was that apart from a weekly salary Metro seemed to have nothing better to offer her than a guest-starring spot in a ghastly cowboy comedy variously billed as *Callaway Went Thataway* and *The Star Said No*, a title line she would have been well advised to echo, followed as it was by a longer role in an equally dire Larry Parks romance called *Love Is Better Than Ever*. This at least had the advantage of being directed by Stanley Donen in between his two great Metromusical successes with *On the Town* and *Singin' in the Rain*. Away from those, however, and despite the off-screen romance with Liz, he seemed totally unable to coax any kind of a performance out of her, and the result was a desperately strained saga of a dancing teacher from New Haven falling for a talent agent in the big city.

During the shooting, Taylor retired to hospital for several days with an incipient ulcer. This was the first of many occasions when an unhappy or uneasy private and professional life would lead her to seek the refuge of the Cedars of Lebanon. She recovered, but the film was struck down by a demand for Larry Parks to appear before the UnAmerican Affairs Committee on charges of Communism. Metro then nervously shelved the whole sorry mess for more than a year, before releasing it as if by accident as the bottom half of an undistinguished double-bill. Having seen their own star turned into an actress by George Stevens over at Paramount during *A Place in the Sun*, the studio now seemed determined to prove that the whole thing had been an accident and that Taylor really couldn't do it at all. Moreover the nightclub coverage was getting to be an embarrassment, as were claims that Liz had destroyed at least one happy marriage apart from her own. That none of these was actually true, since the Donens had anyway been headed for the rocks and there

With her father
on the set of
*Love is Better
Than Ever*
(1952), a
somewhat
ironic title at
the time.

was considerable evidence to support her case against
Hilton even if this hadn't come out in court, was sadly not
the issue in a town and an industry still dominated by its
gossip-column attitudes and its press reviews. The feeling
was growing that Liz had developed into an uninteresting
adult actress and a morally unsafe young woman. On the
other hand her movies were still making money, and Dore
Schary, who was now replacing Louis B. Mayer at the
head of Metro, still thought of her as studio property.

Taylor herself still thought of MGM as her only real
home. When at this time Howard Hughes tried to woo her
away with the promise of a million-dollar contract for six
films, the tricky clause being that she had to marry him as
well, her refusal was immediate. Instead, she even agreed

to the kind of exile which Metro now imposed by sending her to England for the filming of *Ivanhoe*, though admittedly not without a struggle. Still having no wish to be separated from Donen (though that was exactly why she was being sent abroad), as a professional she also recognized that *Ivanhoe* was a pretty terrible script in which the female parts were barely worth having and in which she would have to fight Joan Fontaine for what little interest there was in them. Moreover she was again cast opposite Robert Taylor, and the last time the two Taylors had been packaged off to England by Metro the result had been *Conspirator*; a mere two years later, who needed to make that mistake again?

Nevertheless the studio prevailed, largely by threatening to hand the role on to Deborah Kerr, and Taylor got her own back by giving one of her dead-behind-the-eyes performances in which most of the acting is done by her costumes. When finally required to go to the stake, having lost her Ivanhoe to Joan Fontaine, she wore, as one critic noted, the mildly irritated look of a girl who has been stood up on a fairly important date.

As usual on a Taylor location, however, what was happening behind the cameras was of considerably more interest. Early in the shooting she began seeing a good deal of Michael Wilding, who was at work on a nearby sound stage and whom she'd first met briefly during her earlier London visit for *Conspirator*. At forty, Wilding was just twice her age and, decided Liz, exactly what she now needed: a graceful gentleman actor to bring a little dignity if not a lot of talent into her already over-publicized and under-organized private life. The fact that Wilding was currently having an affair with Marlene Dietrich was no real problem, since neither of them had any intention of marriage; what was more of a problem was that Wilding was then at the height of his career as an English film star and locked into a twenty-year contract with Herbert Wilcox, who was regularly casting him as the elegant screen partner of his wife Anna Neagle in a series of cascadingly gracious British romantic comedies.

Taylor made her case perfectly clear: 'Michael represented tranquility, security and maturity, all the things I needed in myself . . . unfortunately you can't get them by just touching somebody else.' That discovery, however, was only to come two children and five years later; in the meantime, Wilding had to be eased out of a totally English life and moved to California, since there were now strong signs that Metro wanted to renew their contract with Liz on a second seven-year plan which would gradually raise her income to five thousand dollars a week. Quite why Wilding agreed to a marriage and a move which was to prove the total destruction of his career is less clear. Never a dedicated actor, he was perhaps already bored with what promised to be an everlasting if profitable screen partnership with Anna Neagle; his old friend and rival Stewart Granger had just made the move to California with Jean Simmons, and Wilding possibly saw his future there too, though without the firm evidence of a studio contract. Most of his English friends, not least Mr and Mrs Wilcox, were appalled, recognizing rightly in Michael an altogether too casual and unambitious figure to survive the Hollywood machine. Even Liz later noted that it was almost impossible to remember being married to him at all. In his life, as in his work, Wilding traded on a kind of gentle charm which proved instantly unmemorable, but there was something in his laid-back, paternal, Home Counties charm which now seemed to be what Taylor was looking for after the hurly-burly of her American romantic entanglements. He represented a kind of security, though ironically one which was to be immediately destroyed by her determination to take him back to America after their marriage at Caxton Hall in the early February of 1952, just before her twentieth birthday.

Those who thought the marriage wouldn't work could have filled Westminster Abbey itself, and right up to the wedding day Wilding was still seen around town with Dietrich while Taylor was on a different nightclub circuit escorted by an already haggard Montgomery Clift in a relationship that was to run on through many of her more formal alliances. Bridal photographs showed a grittily radiant Taylor and an already weary Wilding, who had apparently only just woken up to the appalling professional and financial situation that Liz was creating for him. Like Esther Williams, famous for being a star only when wet, Wilding was really only a star when squiring Anna Neagle in their series of clenched Mayfair and Park Lane affairs. Now he had unilaterally broken the Wilcox contract in order to marry Taylor, was anyway unable to take money abroad under contemporary currency restrictions, and had no promise of a job in California, where his over-English films remained largely unseen and unknown. True, such friends as James Mason and Stewart Granger had also run into little local difficulties when uprooting post-war English careers for the glitter of California, but they at least had the sense to leave London with something more than a wife to guarantee their American employment.

Yet Taylor was happily still a force to be reckoned with at Metro's contract department. Her recent films might have been critically unmemorable, but all of them had made money at the box-office and she remained a cherished property. Moreover her second marriage neatly coincided with the moment when, for the first time in seven years, she was actually in a strong bargaining position: her first contract with MGM was now at an end, and there were still enough other studios eager to poach her for Taylor to be able to name her own terms. She could, easily enough, go elsewhere; she might even have

The second wedding: to Michael Wilding, London, February 1952.

managed to form her own production company. Instead, she merely listed her requirements: a new five-year contract at five thousand dollars a week, a deal whereby her mother would still be retained as her official minder at three hundred dollars a week, and a further deal whereby Wilding would be guaranteed three thousand dollars a week for three years.

Metro agreed to all of that, and it was therefore unexpected that Taylor's second marriage should have started with the first real money troubles of her young life. But Wilding left London with virtually nothing, having used what there was of his Wilcox earnings to half-settle a considerable tax debt; and soon after they arrived in California, Liz got pregnant. This had, she said, been one of her principal reasons for becoming Mrs Wilding, but it did not endear her to the studio since they were already starting to shoot her next picture, a routine if desperately unimaginative glossy comedy called *The Girl Who Had Everything*, in which she again managed to bring her limited acting skills to bear on a deeply underwritten character.

Wilding meanwhile, in a rare burst of decisive rebellion, turned down his first Metro assignment (a horror called *Latin Lovers*) and was immediately put on unsalaried suspension, a condition unforeseen when Taylor negotiated his contract but one under which he was in fact to spend the majority of his time with the studio. The happy couple had also just bought a $150,000 house in the Hollywood hills of which about half the cost had been raised by Taylor cashing in her child-star money, earned and banked at a time early in her career when she didn't have a husband or baby to worry about. The rest of the house money she had to borrow from the studio, thereby immediately putting herself back in their total control.

Press photographs of Mr and Mrs Michael Wilding in the first flush of pregnancy showed them curled up with a biography of the Barrymores, as if intending to become the First Family for a whole new generation of moviegoers; the truth was that they were a couple of actors in studio trouble, with a serious cash crisis and a baby on the way.

The Girl Who Had Everything (1953).

63

Mother Superior

'Elizabeth Taylor in *Giant* is
compounded of equal parts of
fervour and Ferber' *New York
Herald Tribune*

The Girl Who Had Everything was an ironic title for a girl who now had an unemployed husband and a studio overdraft, but it did at least give Liz top billing (something she had been denied in the medieval western that was *Ivanhoe* for obvious titular reasons) and the line that should perhaps eventually be engraved on her monument: 'I shall,' she tells her lawyer father William Powell solemnly, 'make my own mistakes.'

One of those was of course this film, which gave her everything but a decent script and a good director. The vehicle had proved sturdy enough for Norma Shearer, Lionel Barrymore and Clark Gable as *A Free Soul* back in 1931, but Powell and Fernando Lamas were by no means quite the same casting, and Taylor's increasingly evident pregnancy did not help the camera angles. Indeed as soon as the shooting finished, MGM took her off salary altogether until the baby was born and her figure could get back to normal, a gesture which when taken together with Wilding's continued suspension did not exactly endear the expectant couple to their studio employers or improve their financial prospects.

Around the time of her twenty-first birthday, already the survivor of a decade in movies, Elizabeth was now in a kind of enforced retirement: while other careers, notably those of Grace Kelly and Marilyn Monroe, began to come into focus, hers drifted into a series of 'wife and mother' profiles which suggested that she was now prepared to sacrifice work altogether in order to bring up a Wilding family. The truth was as usual considerably more complex: though she did indeed badly want Wilding's children, she was already finding him less than sparkling as a companion. Lacking in both talent and ready cash, one or other of which had always been her requirement in the past, he was proving an amiable escort and far too well-mannered to cause any of the Hilton troubles, but not exactly the answer to her dream of affluent domesticity. She therefore had to get back to work as soon as possible after the birth of their first child in January 1953, an event marked by the first of what were to become ritual 'Liz in Baby Drama' headlines when the baby had to be delivered by Caesarean section.

But by now she had learnt enough to hold out for a half-

At London Airport in 1954 with the first of her Wilding children.

way decent script: during her pregnancy she'd lost *Young Bess* to Jean Simmons, and on her recovery had the sense to reject *All the Brothers Were Valiant* on the grounds that she'd already made it about three times under other titles. The film that would really have re-established her, *Roman Holiday*, was then with Frank Capra who wanted Liz for the princess opposite Cary Grant; when, however, it got taken over by William Wyler, those roles went to Audrey Hepburn and Gregory Peck, leaving Taylor still on studio suspension until, for once, her career was radically altered by the illness of someone other than herself.

It was during the filming of *Elephant Walk* on location amid the heat and humidity of Ceylon that Vivien Leigh suffered the worst of the nervous breakdowns that were to limit and ultimately destroy her later career, and this one was not much helped by the fact that her co-star in the movie was Peter Finch with whom she was then having a disastrous affair during her doomed marriage to Olivier. Flown to Hollywood, where it was hoped she would recover enough to shoot the interiors, Leigh sank into a spell of near-total madness and it became clear to Paramount that they were in deep trouble unless they could find a replacement very quickly indeed, one moreover who could actually resemble Leigh in the location long-shots since there was no economic possibility of taking the whole picture back to Ceylon for a new start.

Taylor resembled Leigh in height and build, was totally available and had lost the fifty pounds she'd gained in pregnancy; true, she was technically still on suspension for having rejected *All the Brothers Were Valiant*, but once MGM realized how badly Paramount needed her services as a Leigh replacement they rapidly took her back into the fold, having first ascertained that the rival studio would pay $150,000 for the contract loan, plus another $3,000 per day for delaying any other project which MGM might want to throw Taylor into. And that would of course be paid direct to the studio, which in order to claim its windfall merely had to put Liz back on her usual $5,000 salary.

Thus it was that she got to play the tea-planter's wife in a sultry tale of illicit romance, cholera epidemics, marauding elephants and indoor polo. Several critics

With Peter Finch and Michael Wilding on the set of Elephant Walk (1954); 'Miss Taylor as the young wife is petulant and smug, and Mr Finch as the husband is just plain bad.' New York Times

thought they could see Vivien Leigh in the final cut, not only in the location long-shots where of course they could, but also as a ghostly presence hovering over Taylor's shoulder as she attempted none too successfully to represent something more than yet another pretty young colonial wife caught up in some sort of quandary. And although Vivien was almost twenty years the elder of the two, both women had indeed come to represent for Hollywood an image very different from that of the Cleopatra they would both immortalize in bad movies: both also stood for a kind of graciously frozen English grace under pressure, in which line of work they were only ever challenged by the even chillier Grace Kelly, who managed on occasion from the other side of the Atlantic to appear to have come from still more Home Counties than either of them. It wasn't that either Leigh, from an Anglo-Indian background, or Taylor after long years in California were especially English, merely that they managed supremely to behave on screen the way thousands of Americans always wanted the British to behave.

But *Elephant Walk* that had been nothing but disastrous for Leigh nearly ended up that way for Taylor, too; after the studio shooting was complete and the locations had been more or less adequately matched, she spent a day posing with Finch for some production stills, at the end of which a wind machine broke and shot a pellet of metal into her eye-socket, where it duly rusted, sending her once again into hospital, this time with a fair chance of going blind in one eye.

That danger averted by some rapid surgery, Taylor returned to MGM and her Wilding family, painfully aware that even standing in for Vivien Leigh had not restored her listless career. In fact she was still not even sure that she wanted a career on the terms it was currently being offered, but as Wilding's own resolutely refused to take off in a town where Anna Neagle escorts were not exactly at a premium, money was urgently needed. Meanwhile the work itself was proving to be her only escape from a marriage which, though by no means as tortured or unhappy as her first, was nevertheless already in some peril of expiry through a mix of boredom and inertia. Wilding in private life was every bit as nice and very

Hollywood private lives: with Michael Wilding junior at a Jane Powell children's party.

nearly as boring as he always appeared on screen, and Taylor was rapidly tiring of the notion that what she most needed in her life was a father figure for herself as well as her children.

As far as her career was concerned, its major public-relations problem at this time had to do with her screen image which managed to appear both WASP and Yuppie before either of those notions had been formally invented; this meant that her usual casting was strictly limited to nice young matrons in some elegant kind of social or geographic trauma, and these were not presently the most exciting roles around. Magazines of the day were full of picture-profiles in which an apparently radiant Liz droned on about the joys of motherhood: but she was patently not Debbie Reynolds (as a later battle over Eddie Fisher would indicate), and being already twice married by the age of twenty somehow denied her access to Mother of the Year awards. Moreover, those who took any professional interest at all in the development of her career as an actress, and there were as usual precious few, now found it hard to reconcile a suddenly domestic Mrs Wilding with the Taylor who had done her best screen work in the dangerously edgy and extramarital *Place in the Sun*.

Undeterred by such professional considerations, and

doubtless aware that she now lacked both the energy and the economic resources for any sustained suspension battles, MGM merely kept her filed under 'looks lovely, acts a little' and duly cast her in *Rhapsody*, where once again she was required to sleepwalk through her poor-little-rich-girl routine while Vittorio Gassman played the violin and audiences all over the world vaguely wondered whatever had happened to keep Joan Crawford and John Garfield from the action.

Even in 1953 a tears-and-torment drama such as this was looking remarkably dated, and Liz in her Taylor-Dummy mood was unable to retrieve a script of stunning banality which required Michael Chekhov, late of the Moscow Art Theatre, to intone, 'There can be no great art without discipline and no discipline without sacrifice.' But it seemed as though MGM were determined to distance and dislocate Elizabeth from her natural career progression; if she wanted to play wife and mother then they were in no hurry to find her roles which might actually further her talent as an actress; she was, after all, still studio property, albeit faintly less valuable now she came complete with husband and family instead of as everyone's favourite sexy daughter.

Yet Taylor knew how badly she needed a good script: in these early 1950s she fought her studio unsuccessfully for the Ava Gardner role in *The Barefoot Contessa* and the Susan Hayward part in *I'll Cry Tomorrow*, only to end up being sent back into English exile for the *Beau Brummell* with which the costume and wooden-dialogue departments had decided to follow up their triumph on *Ivanhoe* in the previous year. The film achieved a kind of immortality by becoming the least suitable ever to have been set before the Queen at a Royal Film Performance (since it featured Robert Morley as one of her mad ancestors attempting to strangle Peter Ustinov as the future George IV), and even Taylor later noted that 'whenever it comes on television I have to switch over', while Stewart Granger in the title role could remember mainly that Liz endeared herself to him by yawning in the face of the German director, Curtis Bernhardt, whenever he attempted to instruct her in the intricacies of her role as the beautiful Lady Patricia. Neither of the two stars much

'Most of the performers in *Beau Brummell* [1954] are china figures, including Taylor as an eligible maiden of fashion' *New York Herald Tribune*; It was just embarrassing.' *Elizabeth Taylor*

cared for being away from Hollywood, where they had left those they most loved (at this time Jean Simmons and Michael Wilding), and neither much cared for the film which C. A. Lejeune summarized simply enough as 'horrid history' while the *New York Times* reckoned Taylor 'still decorative but something less than useful as a heroine'.

For the third film in a row, Taylor was cast here as the woman who lost her man (in fact no fewer than four men were lost to her in *Rhapsody* and *Elephant Walk*, in most cases because they rejected her towards the last reel), thereby somewhat damaging her image as one of Hollywood's most desirable women. 'Beau Bloomer' and 'Bore Brummell' were some of the less admiring titles given the movie by London critics, while Taylor was less than delighted to discover later that she had been used as a last-minute replacement for Eleanor Parker, with whom

Granger had previously buckled his swash through another costumed yawner called *Scaramouche*. But it was a film critic on *Variety* who best summarized her essential problem on screen as in life at this time: 'Miss Taylor,' he noted memorably, 'is a victim of motivation obscurity.'

The Wilding alliance which had started out as that of a father and daughter was rapidly drifting into that of a brother and sister and not always on the best of terms. Michael patently had neither the ambition nor the talent nor even the energy to take Hollywood by storm ('It will never understand you,' his old mentor Herbert Wilcox had warned him at the outset, 'and you will never understand it', while Liz was more blunt: 'The trouble with you,' she told him when the economic going began to get rough, 'is that you're so goddamn English') and for his part Wilding found it almost impossible to appreciate that for his wife, however hard she tried to deny it in moments of high maternity, a life in film was still the only one worth having.

Work started to separate them for long periods: Wilding's tax troubles were ironically such that he was unable to return to his beloved England while Liz was there on *Beau Brummell*, and after a couple of years of marriage what they now mainly had in common was their son and the fact that one or other of them was usually on studio suspension having had a row about the nature or location address of a script. The difference was that where Liz was always taken back after the row, since Metro still regarded her as a wilful daughter, Wilding was not exactly their idea of an adopted son-in-law and they could get along just fine without him.

Wilding was actually happiest when he wasn't even trying to work: whether painting large portraits of Liz or looking after their child or drifting around Santa Monica with such old Pinewood friends and fellow-exiles as Stewart Granger and James Mason, expressing mild horror at the social habits and mentalities of the Hollywood natives with whom Liz was more inclined to side, he not only lacked but also failed ever to understand the odd mix of absorption, rage and nervous energy which characterized his second wife in her attitude to a film industry that was still all she had ever really known.

Scott Fitzgerald once said that he accepted Hollywood with all the resignation of a ghost assigned to a haunted house, and that was evidently much how Wilding felt about it; but for Liz the haunted house was still full of people who had to be beaten into acceptance of her talent as an actress, not that this had been much in evidence of late, or at the very least of her rights as a star, and the only way to achieve that was to keep working. Besides, she still needed the money; Wilding was living on suspension as often as not and his earnings remained about a tenth of hers even at the best of times. She was now on about two hundred thousand dollars a year from Metro, but fifteen per cent of that went to managers and agents and another sixty per cent was withheld for tax. Then there were the repayments to Metro on the money she and Wilding had borrowed to buy their house, plus a staff of cook, nanny, housekeeper and gardener to support, while much of what was left over went on medical bills, since she was by now plagued with sciatica among other ailments. All of which was how Taylor came to spend most of the Wilding marriage up to her ears in debt, a situation MGM took no steps to alter since it meant that she was less than usually troublesome about scripts and co-stars, albeit still often troublesome enough.

Within a year of the birth of her first son she had made three undistinguished movies (*Elephant Walk*, *Rhapsody* and *Beau Brummell*) and she now went straight on to a fourth, which, though no more loved by the critics, did at least rate a place alongside *National Velvet* and *A Place in the Sun* in Taylor's own list of important movies: 'Most of the films I did in that period have sort of blanked out in my mind because they were so distasteful to me: but rather curiously a not-so-good picture called *The Last Time I Saw Paris* first convinced me that I wanted to be an actress instead of just yawning my way through parts. That girl was offbeat with mercurial flashes of instability – more than just glib dialogue.'

The 'girl' was in fact a thinly disguised portrait of Zelda Fitzgerald, and the movie was based on her husband Scott's *Babylon Revisited*, the story of a novelist on the bottle whose wife eventually dies of pneumonia. 'Thin, trite, glossy and pedestrian', thought the *New York*

With Van
Johnson in *The
Last Time I
Saw Paris*
(1954); 'a not-
so-good
picture, but
oddly enough it
was the one
that first
convinced me I
wanted to be
an actress
instead of just
yawning my
way through
parts.'
*Elizabeth
Taylor*

Times, and the central problem with Richard Brooks's film was perhaps that its casting required audiences to accept Van Johnson as the award-winning author based on Fitzgerald himself. But Taylor was right to recognize in her own performance something altogether different, more adult and intriguing, than any of her recent work. In that sense, if not at the box-office or in the review columns, *The Last Time I Saw Paris* was the natural successor to the *Place in the Sun* she had made seven films and three years and one child and one husband earlier, and in its own lugubrious, sub-literary, alcoholic and soap-operatic way it actually marked a turning-point in her career: at twenty-two she seemed suddenly to have grown up on camera, and even the *New Yorker* had to acknowledge that its verdict on the last Taylor/Johnson partnership in *The Big Hangover* ('Miss Taylor is beautiful and cannot act, which puts her one up on Mr Johnson') would now have to be slightly amended. *The Last Time I Saw Paris* left no heartstring untugged, from the classic Jerome Kern title song to a shot of Taylor dying in a Parisian snowstorm, blood red against the white background, but it established another tenet of her future career: she was very often from now on to emerge at her best from the worst possible surroundings.

In the meantime there was an unusual year-long pause in her career while she had the second of her Wilding children and moved to a larger and even more unaffordable house in the Hollywood hills, accompanied as ever by the faithful Peggy Rutledge, her secretary since the days of the Nicky Hilton fiasco, and an exotic menagerie of dogs and cats several of whom, noted an appalled visitor, had begun to chew their way through carpets and bedclothes in what was to be a regular feature of the Taylor lifestyle as she moved through various marriages, often managing to keep the pets longer than the partners.

Taylor's year out of action in the very middle of the 1950s was not that long, but it allowed both Grace Kelly and Marilyn Monroe to confirm their box-office leads over her at precisely the moment when the old studio structure (of which she rather than either of them was the last star daughter) was falling apart in the face of television and increased European competition. By the time Taylor got back to Metro in 1955, again the proud mother of a Wilding son but increasingly irritated at her husband's lackadaisical attitude towards movie- and money-making and increasingly determined to build on the acting skills she had begun to teach herself during *The Last Time I Saw Paris*, it was to discover that once again a new studio boss (this time Benny Thau) had not the remotest idea what to do with her.

Only seven actors were by now left on the roster of the studio that had once proudly boasted of 'more stars than are in the heavens'; apart from the Taylors, Elizabeth and Robert, they were Grace Kelly, Ava Gardner, Cyd Charisse, Leslie Caron and Debbie Reynolds. Moreover that year Metro was to release barely twenty pictures, less than half the number they had been making on the lot when Liz first joined them a decade earlier. So she was now effectively back to work in a ghost town, and soon realized that she would have to get out of it; if not by abandoning the contract that was still her only claim to any kind of financial survival, then at least by a loan-out to another studio where something worthwhile might be going on. To have stayed within the Metro gates at this time would have been to invite the same fate as Clark Gable, once King of the studio but recently thrown out on his ear after playing loyally through nine years of MGM rubbish which had more or less managed to undo all the glory of his pre-war career.

Looking around a rapidly shrinking Hollywood, it didn't take Taylor long to find what she needed: over at Warners, her old *Place in the Sun* mentor George Stevens (who had devoted the intervening five years to just one other Oscar-winner, *Shane*) was starting pre-production on what promised to be the epic of the year. *Giant* was a suitably huge treatment of Edna Ferber's bestseller about the mega-rich ranchers and oil kings of Texas, seen across a thirty-year span of domestic drama and state history; it was in fact to be the forerunner of (and inspiration for) the television serial hit of the 1980s, *Dallas*, which even borrowed the initials of the James Dean figure (Jett Rink) for its central villain.

For the newly wide screen, Rock Hudson was to play the rancher-baron paterfamilias, with James Dean, in the third and last of the films that were to make him a teen legend, as the farmhand who strikes oil. The part of Hudson's wife, who had to age from a child-bride of eighteen to the fifty-year-old mother of Dennis Hopper and Carroll Baker, had already been offered to Grace Kelly, she who had graciously declined most of the scripts with which Taylor had been lumbered of late. That they should have been locked together in a struggle for the same roles during these mid-1950s was perhaps not surprising: apart from an MGM contract, they shared a certain kind of glacial beauty and a background of no-struggle wealth and childhood security very different from that of the conventional rags-to-riches star upbringing.

But the luck of the script draw, which for so long had been against her, was at last back with Elizabeth: since Grace Kelly was at this time by far the hotter of the two MGM princesses in residence, they decided that they wanted to keep her at home, especially as four of her last six pictures had been made on loan-out to other studios. Metro could still afford to live without Taylor for a while, and to Kelly's indignation it was therefore Liz who was dispatched to Marfa, Texas, for what proved to be a long, hot summer.

A lot happened during *Giant*, though unfortunately for cinema-goers most of it took place off the screen; the film itself, in Stevens's careful, laborious treatment, came to resemble some endless wide-screen soap opera from which all the most eventful episodes had been mysteriously deleted. First of all the Wilding marriage, which had been foundering for several months and was only very briefly revived by the birth of their second son, now became a matter of total separation. Michael went back to Europe to try to revive a flagging career with the appalling *Zarak*; his wife meanwhile turned to the gay Rock Hudson for a platonic friendship and then began to find in their co-star James Dean something altogether more sexually exciting.

There is no evidence of an actual affair with Dean, since Taylor only very seldom lived with men to whom she was not either legally married at the time or about to be so, but there's no doubt that she found in his potent, anguished, little-boy-lost stardom a quality that was totally unforthcoming from the stale Wilding marriage, a quality more

'*Giant* [1956] is a timelessly vivid picture that gushes a tawdry tragedy: it is James Dean as the malignant ranch-hand who is the most tangy and corrosive in the film, while Rock Hudson plays the ranch owner and Elizabeth Taylor makes a woman of spirit and sensitivity out of his wife.' *New York Times*

akin to what she was always looking for and failing to find in the equally anguished and juvenile but also gay Montgomery Clift.

Then there was the problem of the director: the George Stevens who had guided her so carefully and lovingly through *A Place in the Sun* half a decade earlier now seemed to regard Taylor with a stern distaste, regarding her as starry and difficult and altogether too prone to a bad back when the shooting got rough. Liz did in fact have sciatica and was also deeply unhappy about the state of her personal life; and when, towards the end of the shooting, her new friend Dean got himself killed at the wheel of his Porsche, Taylor went into a deep nervous depression. It was then that Stevens, already way over budget and behind schedule (he was shooting at a ratio of 24 feet for every one used in the final cut, an extravagance almost unknown even to Hollywood at that time), demanded that she film one last and tricky scene with Hudson, one in fact that she spent largely in tears over Dean, so that what can finally be seen on screen is very often just the back of her head.

Professionally and privately, Dean in *Giant* had fulfilled for Liz much the same function as another great method actor, Montgomery Clift had in *American Tragedy* with the same director. On screen, Dean too represented danger and an alternative to a boringly conventional if wealthy private life; whereas behind the camera he was another of the illicit romances she could never have – not on this occasion because of any homosexuality but simply because his own interests lay elsewhere and she still regarded herself for better or worse as Mrs Michael Wilding. Dean was also to end up, within a few months of their first meeting, as the first of the sudden-death shocks that were from now on to be a regular feature of Taylor's life.

Not surprisingly, she then retreated to hospital for several weeks with a twisted colon, having survived a long and uneasy film, a violent death in her working family and come to terms with the inevitability of a second divorce. The drama of *Giant*, even in its sprawling length and gargantuan width, had as usual nothing to compare with the drama of Taylor.

Todd Almighty

'Miss Taylor is unimpeachable at suggesting the poor little rich girl of Hollywood fable' *Sight & Sound*

Though their relationship was now severely strained by Stevens's single-minded, obsessive dedication to the art of making movies and Taylor's habit of retiring to bed in times of emotional or physical crisis ('She has every qualification for stardom,' said the director during one of these, 'except the ability to concentrate') he had once again managed to kick-start her ailing career. Like *A Place in the Sun*, *Giant* was to prove a giant box-office money-maker, grossing seven million dollars in the year of its first release, and Liz's youth-to-old-age performance in it, while staid and overly theatrical by turns, nonetheless put her back into a position of commercial power. She was playing the leading female role in the leading picture of the year at a time when those things still mattered, and she was by now all of twenty-three.

Though she had sworn never again to work for Stevens, a vow she kept, much to his amazement, when in 1965 he offered a five-times-married lady the role of Mary Magdelene in *The Greatest Story Ever Told*, the director had given her a taste for epics which was to carry forward into 1956 with *Raintree County*: this was to have a budget of five million dollars, the highest ever funded by MGM, and Taylor's co-star in place of James Dean was to be her other anguished, moody, Methody, self-destructive friend Montgomery Clift.

First, however, there was the problem of the Wilding marriage to be sorted out: this was now clearly at an end, as even Taylor began giving interviews emphasizing the difficulties of being married to a 'goddamn Englishman' who refused ever to lose his temper. Taylor was now way beyond her quest for respectable maternity and the wifely virtues: she had played the role of Mrs Wilding for a good four years, found it unrewarding maritally, commercially and artistically, and was more than ready to be recast in a more exciting alliance if she could find one. Meanwhile all the gossip columnists were eagerly reporting that Wilding had filled his home with glamour girls during Taylor's Texan stay on *Giant*; all the gossip columnists, that is, bar Hedda Hopper who, never a writer to let truth get in the way of a deadline, came up with a vastly more intriguing theory as to the breakdown of the marriage. Wilding, she solemnly announced to her aghast mid-1950s readers,

had for several years been living in a secret homosexual relationship with Stewart Granger, another English expatriate actor and therefore likely in Miss Hopper's view to have been getting up to nasty foreign habits. Granger, whose career was then still in rather better shape than Wilding's, decided not to go to the trouble of a lawsuit, but Wilding went ahead and extracted substantial damages as well as a grovelling apology from Hopper, who admitted that she had written 'in a malicious and wanton fashion' and that there was no word of truth in the allegation.

It was, however, true that Wilding's marriage was over in all but official appearances: a gentle, kindly, graceful man, he had no desire for a noisy or abrupt separation, being apparently content to drift amicably into a separate bedroom and live on with Taylor as a kind of guardian brother for several months more. They were indeed still giving parties together, and a regular guest was Montgomery Clift until one horrendous night during the shooting of *Raintree County* when, after dinner at the Wildings, Clift crashed his car into a telegraph pole, smashing his head into the steering wheel so badly that his friend Kevin McCarthy, driving the car in front to guide Clift home, assumed he had been killed instantaneously.

Taylor, coming up well in a crisis as ever, ran to where the crash was, cradled Clift in her arms for nearly an hour and then fought off several press photographers with language which managed to shock even them. In hospital, it became clear that Clift was going to live but would need major plastic surgery and weeks if not months to recover. MGM, with their five-million-dollar investment in *Raintree County* to protect, immediately if tastelessly announced that they would be recasting the Clift role and reshooting the early scenes accordingly. Again, it was Taylor who behaved best in the crisis: if, she said, they were planning to recast Clift's role, then they would also have to recast hers, since she was certainly not going to finish the film without her old friend, however long it took for him to recover.

What she knew very well, as she sat for hours beside Clift's hospital bed, was that she now had the studio over a barrel: she and she alone was the bankable star in *Raintree County*, and, quite apart from the problem of recasting not one but two central roles, they were too far down the line to finish it without her. Grudgingly, furiously, MGM announced that there would be a hiatus of eight weeks before shooting resumed with the original cast.

Midway through the enforced break, which she spent largely nursing Clift back on to his feet and perfecting a deep-Southern accent which was to come in useful not only for *Raintree County* but also the later and vastly better *Cat on a Hot Tin Roof*, Taylor and Wilding were invited to a party on a yacht chartered by the man who was to be her next husband, Avrom Goldenborgen or (as he was better known) Mike Todd. Considerably older than Taylor, older even than Wilding, Todd was then at the height of his mercurial career, having just completed post-production on the film that was to be his one enduring claim to fame, *Around the World in Eighty Days*, an all-star travelogue in which Taylor was about the only Hollywood resident not to have been given a small role.

Here was another father-figure Michael, but one so totally different from Wilding that they might have come from different planets. A stubby, stocky, cigar-chewing opportunist whose career had veered from vast wealth to total disaster and back again with amazing regularity, Todd was now on the verge of his fiftieth birthday, loosely engaged to Evelyn Keyes but bowled over by his first sight of Taylor on that yacht. Almost at once, they became a couple: she gave him class, he gave her huge diamonds and a kind of tough energy that had been totally unforthcoming from her two previous husbands. Todd lacked the elegance and charm of Wilding, just as he lacked the secure wealth of Hilton: he was a street fighter who had started out as the producer of burlesque and strip shows in Chicago (one of which was heavily advertised locally as 'not Shakespeare but it's Laffs') and endured a catastrophic liaison with Orson Welles during which a stage version of *Around the World* had lost several million pre-war dollars.

Surviving that, two official bankruptcies and two marriages (one to the actress Joan Blondell, another to a woman who had died in mysterious circumstances soon after being sued by him for mental cruelty), Todd had finished up in California with a wide-screen projection device known as Todd-AO and a few more million dollars, mainly belonging to others, which he had now invested in the make-or-break filming of *Around the World*. In business and in private he was, if not direct, then at least outspoken: 'From now on,' he told Taylor soon after their first meeting, 'you will fuck nobody but me' – not an instruction that was likely ever to have passed the lips of Michael Wilding.

Apart from a tremendous and mutual sexual attraction, and the prospect of a third marriage for them both, Todd saw in Elizabeth Taylor something more: he saw an extremely valuable property coming on to the open market at the end of the Metro-Wilding years, one moreover that had never been properly advertised. And if there was anything Todd really knew, it was advertising. He now had an expensive movie to sell all over the world, at a series of gala premieres where Taylor would look good and photogenic on his arm. It was at one of these, all of thirty years ago, that I met him for the first and last time, but it was an instructive occasion: after the West End opening of *Around the World*, he and Liz invited the families of all the cast and crew to a party at the Battersea Pleasure Gardens which they had hired for the night. Being an English midsummer it was of course pouring with rain; foreseeing that, Todd had somehow acquired hundreds if not thousands of the then brand-new plastic

raincoats, and as he stood at the Battersea gates handing them out, I vividly remember him wondering aloud, not about his movie or its critical or public reception in Britain, but about plastic macs, whether there was any future in them and if so whether he should maybe try for a franchise.

As he now set about the marketing of his movie and his new mistress as a superstar divorced from any studio publicity machine for the first time, Todd happened to hit the precise moment when Grace Kelly was about to move into a regal Monagesque retirement, and Taylor could get back into the spotlight as the natural Queen by birthright of a Hollywood where Marilyn Monroe was still regarded as an upstart. Todd heightened Taylor's sex appeal but he managed to keep her respectable enough for family audiences: she would after all be divorcing Wilding before marrying him, and the fact that they were living together in the meantime was not one which, in 1956, the gossip columnists were prepared to explore on account of

Taylor's still carefully preserved celluloid royalty.

In the time it took to stop being Mrs Michael Wilding and start being Mrs Michael Todd, the electric lightbulbs surrounding Liz's name grew several thousand volts brighter, and it was Todd who knew how to control that particular current: with him and because of him, she became a more dangerous and intriguing figure. He brought her out of the dark ages of studio contracts and domestic marriages and established her as one of the great showbiz attractions of the middle 1950s; her mother's refined horror at the way Todd persisted in sticking his hand down her daughter's cleavage while referring proprietorially to his 'good Jewish girl' (a religion in which Liz soon started to take instruction) was but a small price to pay for such a professional transformation.

The fact that her private life was now getting vastly more dynamic, as reflected by the gossip columns which suddenly acquired a fresh interest, was probably just as well since her working life was still rooted in worthy but dull epics. *Raintree County*, on which shooting restarted as soon as Clift had recovered from his car smash, was a marathon yawner which reached the wide screen at nearly three and a half hours but lacked even the guiding intellect of George Stevens on *Giant*. Here, Edward Dmytryk attempted against a background of the American Civil War to tell of 'the bone and marrow of human existence, man's eternal struggle for happiness and the tumult that almost disunited the United States'. What he in fact ended up with was a kind of deep-Southern western, with Montgomery Clift as the anguished hero torn between Taylor, as the wife driven mad by fears that she might have negro blood in her, and Eva Marie Saint, as the childhood sweetheart to whom he eventually returns after what seem like several hundred years of screen time have elapsed.

Raintree County did, however, win Taylor her first-ever Oscar nomination, after a campaign which she insisted was to be run on merit rather than the 'Macchiavellian machinations' of her future husband. For all that, Todd sent a form-letter around Hollywood soliciting support for her performance as the demented southern belle, though in the event she was beaten by Joanne

Woodward for another mad lady in *The Three Faces of Eve*. In the rather less than 24 months that elapsed between the shooting of *Raintree County* and its Oscar night, Taylor had divorced Wilding, suffered another long hospital incarceration, married Todd, had his child and become his widow – all before her twenty-sixth birthday. Her life was still nothing if not eventful.

'The film gives evidence of being outfitted with every extravagance except a script,' thought Bosley Crowther, and the same could well have been true of Taylor's off-screen existence, which now took on a kind of manic intensity: the day after she announced her separation from Wilding, who seemed to greet the news with a resignation amounting almost to relief that a noisy period in his life was drawing to a close, Todd announced that he would henceforth be pressing his suit with a view to marriage just as soon as the law would permit. He then presented Liz with several diamonds and a painting which uncharitable observers thought was already in the Taylor art-collecting family, before whisking her around the world with *Around the World*, which won an Acadamy Award for best picture, for its various international premieres. By the end of 1956 she was promising retirement from the screen to have Todd's children, describing her future husband as 'an extremely fascinating man who makes me feel very old' – which, considering he was just twice her age, must have been meant as a compliment.

Going to the Bahamas that winter, she slipped down the staircase of a yacht, which meant a five-hour operation for the removal of three spinal discs and trouble with her back for the next thirty years. She spent Christmas in hospital, where Todd had her meals sent in from a neighbouring restaurant; and intriguingly the hospital was in New York, which Todd had always regarded as, after Chicago, his natural home. Taylor was not only leaving Wilding for him, she was also leaving California, vowing simply to follow Todd wherever around the world his ambition to be the last of the mogul emperors might take him.

First, however, there was the divorce to get: that was granted in Acapulco on 30 January, with Wilding

Mr and Mrs Mike Todd with Oscar (his).

courteously agreeing to fly down so that matters might be finalized as rapidly as possible. Two days later, at the Mexican seaside villa of some friends, Liz became Mrs Michael Todd: her wedding gifts were another diamond ring and a couple of cinemas in downtown Chicago, while the attendants were (as best man) Todd's greatest friend Eddie Fisher and (as matron of honour) his then wife Debbie Reynolds.

The new Todds still had *Around the World* and *Raintree County* to finish selling, but after that Liz solemnly announced that she would be 'retiring from the commodity known as Elizabeth Taylor'; two failed marriages had, she said, taught her that a career and a family could not successfully be combined. Moreover acting had begun to bore her, and what Todd was offering for the first time in fifteen years was a passport out of California. He even took her to Moscow, where several fans enquired fondly after Deanna Durbin, whose films were at that time still the only American ones widely visible behind the Iron Curtain. She also caught a glimpse of Mr Krushchev whom she thought had a fascinating face, information she divulged to the *Los Angeles Times* on her return to civilization and another pregnancy.

'Any time this little dame spends outa bed,' said Todd of his new wife, 'is time totally wasted'; but he still had a business to run, and Taylor was now one of its more important assets. For all the flamboyance of his gifts and their travels, Todd had still not achieved anything like long-term financial security. *Around the World* had yet to cover its costs, there was not a lot in the bank ('I've been broke several times but I ain't never been poor'), and soon after the birth of their baby girl he let it be known that his wife would be returning to the movies, not this time on any kind of a studio contract but to the highest bidder for a one-picture deal. The birth itself had not been easy, complicated by Liz's recent spinal operation, and doctors advised Todd that she should have a tubal ligation rather than risk the dangers of another pregnancy: regretfully he allowed the operation, and delighted though they both were with their first and last child (who now joined the two Wilding boys, of whom Liz had been given custody), that seemed to be the end of Taylor's dream of spending the rest of her life surrounded by large numbers of small Todds. She might as well go back to work.

Here there was another problem: Todd's plan to make a lucrative one-picture deal for her overlooked the fact that under the terms of her existing MGM contract she still owed them three more years. In the meantime she spent the second and what was to be the last Christmas of her Todd marriage in hospital, this time having an appendix removed and recovering from a curiously disastrous party at Madison Square Garden which her husband had given in celebration of the first anniversary of *Around the World*. He had invited eighteen thousand people, most of whom ungratefully complained to the press that they had seldom spent a more overcrowded or less enjoyable evening.

Undaunted, Todd acquired a Rolls-Royce and a private aeroplane, renamed the Lucky Liz, and carried on with plans to make a film of *Don Quixote* starring Cantinflas and Fernandel, with Mrs Todd providing some English-language support as Dulcinea. Metro now had a real problem with Liz: they may have held the contract, but Todd held her, and it was perfectly clear that if she was to go on working in the future then it would probably be for him rather than them, whatever the small print specified. Moreover the switch from Elizabeth Taylor to Mrs Todd had come at a particularly awkward moment for the studio since the actress to whom they had routinely been offering all their major roles first, Grace Kelly, had departed for Monaco; this left them with Debbie Reynolds as the only leading lady on their books just as they were about to embark on the filming of *Cat on a Hot Tin Roof*, the Tennessee Williams classic in which Paul Newman was already cast as Brick, with Burl Ives as Big Daddy.

As the royal touring of the Todds ground to a halt with one final *Around the World* stopover in Australia, where they were severely reprimanded in the local press for kissing at a public banquet in the middle of one of the Governor General's less enthralling speeches of welcome (which, considering Todd's usual hands-on behaviour to his wife, was in fact reasonably restrained of him), the studio opened urgent negotiations for the return of Liz.

Aware of the new balance of marital power, the director Richard Brooks at once began talking to Todd about the importance of having Taylor give another of her sensuous poor-little-rich-girl performances as the wife of the homosexual Brick, not that his homosexuality was ever allowed to be manifest in Brooks's inevitably toned-down screenplay. But even allowing for that, Todd realized his wife was now being offered something vastly better than usual; he also realized how desperate Metro were for Taylor, and managed to get an (alas only verbal) agreement out of the studio that at the end of the filming they would immediately release her from the remainder of her contract with no financial penalties of any kind. All that, and one of the best roles written for a woman in post-war

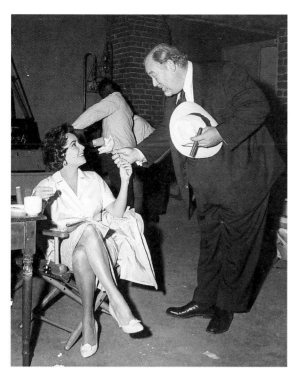

American drama: for the first time in years, perhaps for the first time ever, Liz now had simultaneously a good film and a good marriage, a combination that was to last for all of a fortnight.

When the shooting on *Cat* began, Todd hovered around the set to make sure that his Liz was being looked after correctly: still shaky from the difficult birth of Liza and her later operations, bitterly regretting the tubal ligation that meant she could have no more children ('it's like being killed inside'), she was in a highly-strung condition and not altogether prepared for a film which would demand a level of emotional intensity far greater than that required for the two long, slow and sedate epics which had occupied most of the last four years of her working life.

The first day's shooting was in black-and-white, though that was soon fixed: Todd saw some rushes, agreed with the director that it was a mistake, and even though he had no official connection with the film whatsoever managed in a matter of minutes to convince the Metro executives that they should raise the budget and go immediately into colour. His success there was a useful reminder that, unlike either of Liz's two previous husbands, Todd was an experienced studio negotiator who might in the long term have been able to manage her

With Burl Ives as Big Daddy and Paul Newman as Brick in *Cat on a Hot Tin Roof* (1958): 'a corrosive character study of avarice, Southern pride and seething sexual problems.'

career as it has really never been effectively managed by anyone, even Taylor herself, save in the most lurching kind of manner.

Sadly that was not to be. Two weeks into the shooting of *Cat*, Todd was due in New York for a testimonial dinner at the Friars Club, one of his regular Manhattan homes; Elizabeth had originally planned to be there too, and they were due to fly from Burbank aboard the Lucky Liz. By the Friday night, however, an arduous week in the studio and a bout of flu made her decide reluctantly to stay at home, and early the following morning she was awoken with the news that during a bad thunderstorm the Lucky Liz had crashed into the mountains of New Mexico, killing Todd, his biographer Art Cohn and the two pilots instantly, though such was the intensity of the burning wreckage that Todd could only be identified by his gold wedding ring, which was duly taken home to his widow.

Taylor now went into deep psychiatric shock, at first refusing to believe that the man who had become her husband, lover, agent, manager and maybe above all friend could have disappeared so abruptly from her life, leaving her with their baby and precious little else except the memory of the best sexual and social liaison of her life, one that was also just beginning to develop into a professional partnership when it came to a flaming halt. The funeral in Todd's home town, Chicago, was a nightmare of *Hollywood Babylon* proportions, with bystanders besieging Liz for autographs and desperate journalists solemnly if untruthfully announcing to their readers that she had thrown herself sobbing loudly into her husband's grave. Several battles broke out between Todd and Taylor factions, each of which felt that the other was trying to command the ceremony, and Elizabeth herself duly retreated from the shambles, having managed to persuade her in-laws not to erect a twenty-foot high concrete Oscar over Todd's burial plot, one of their less tasteful notions.

Back in California she went into total retreat, staying in bed for several days; the makers of *Cat* behaved impeccably, shooting around her and exerting no pressure on her to return until, late one afternoon, she was seen on the sidelines of the set and agreed, as much for her own sanity

Mr and Mrs
Mike Todd
going around
the world to
sell his *Around
the World in 80
Days*.

as the picture budget, to return to work on the following
afternoon. Maggie the Cat now proved the saving of Liz:
by hurling herself into the role she managed to take her
mind off Todd's violent death, and as she herself later
noted, 'I was so lucky that I had someone else to become at
a moment when I had gone slightly round the bend with
grief: when I was Maggie was the only time I could
function. The rest of the time I was like a robot.'

Once again, Taylor amazed those working with her (not
least Paul Newman) by giving almost nothing in rehearsal
but then suddenly blazing as the camera rolled, so that her
performance burns off the screen while the others seem
somehow stagey and often unreal by comparison. The
film itself won six major Oscar nominations but not a
single award, thereby neatly confirming the curious divi-
sion among its critics: most resented the fact that the
director Richard Brooks had been forced to soften if not
eliminate entirely the original homosexual theme of Williams's play, while reluctantly admitting that on its own
Hollywood terms it worked very well indeed, a verdict
with which even Williams himself finally concurred.

When she eventually returned to the set, working at first only in the late afternoons, Taylor seemed to find old reserves of strength and courage and above all discipline. A widow a month after her twenty-sixth birthday, mother of three now essentially fatherless children, and with a private life already somewhat scarred by two divorces and the violent crashes that had killed Todd and wounded Clift, the two men who had managed to get closer to her than any others, this period of the *Cat* shooting was for Taylor the breaking point. This was the moment when, if ever, she was going to go the way of Garland and Monroe into the already well-worn tracks of doomed superstars, increasingly unreliable on the set and totally impossible elsewhere.

And yet something deep in Taylor's colder and clearer English background and upbringing forbade that: in times of crisis the puritan ethic has always remained oddly strong in her, and the performance she gave (the best on the film, according to its author) within days and weeks of Todd's death was, if not dramatically award-winning, then emotionally powerful and technically immaculate. Having decided that the film must go on, she turned in a title-role Maggie that stands thirty years later as not only one of her most impressive portrayals but also a sharp reminder of her immense and intense profession-alism under stress: clearly she was not about to disappear into the valley of the dolls.

Nor was she about to stay in total retreat: the final wrap on *Cat* left her with nothing to do and, so much worse after the two brief but orgasmic Todd years, no one to spend her life with apart from her small children. One or two friends rallied round, notably Todd's secretary Dick Hanley who now became her manager, but within a few weeks she was seen around town with a variety of escorts including Arthur Loew and her first husband Nicky Hilton. That in itself was no problem for gossip colum-nists, who readily accepted that Taylor could hardly be expected to disappear off the face of the Hollywood earth simply because she had unfortunately been widowed. The trouble started almost as soon as she was first sighted with the singer Eddie Fisher, although in theory that should have caused no great surprise. Fisher had after all been best man at her last wedding, and as a close friend and almost adoptive son of Todd's it was surely understandable that he should have been at the forefront of those attempting to console Liz. Though there had never been much love lost between her and the current Mrs Fisher, Debbie Reynolds, the bond between their husbands had been so strong that all four were frequently seen around together during Todd's lifetime. Now, however, things were rather different: in August 1958, barely six months after Todd's plane had come down, Fisher was doing a summer cabaret season in a Catskills resort where Taylor joined him, making it instantly and painfully clear to all observers that the two of them were passionately in love.

Thirty years on, it is a little difficult to understand the shock waves that went rippling across America at the news that a pop singer and an already much-married movie star were having an affair in the Catskills, but the reaction was immediate and intense. Over the past few months, Taylor's image had been that of the grieving widow, gallantly carrying on with her career and bringing up her offspring: suddenly American audiences were being asked to recast her in their minds as a dangerous 'other woman', intent on breaking up the marriage of the man who had been her dead husband's greatest friend,

Mrs Mike Todd, soon to be Mrs Eddie Fisher.

and the abrupt switch of roles proved altogether too much for a middle America that still expected at least a facade of moral rectitude from its icons.

The truth was, as usual, a little more complex: Taylor was not actually breaking up the Fisher marriage since that had already been twice headed for the divorce courts, though in a masterly public-relations exercise Debbie did then appear at the door of her house surrounded by small children (one of whom later went on to be the Princess in *Star Wars* and a bestselling author of a book about drug addiction) and nappies and righteous indignation at having her husband 'stolen' from her.

As Taylor now lurched from the black to the scarlet, there was another problem: nobody in her own Hollywood circle expected her to remain celibate forever after Todd, but there was a limit, and a pop singer like Fisher was definitely over it. For all his social and economic failings, Todd had at least been a movie mogul of sorts; Fisher was only at Hollywood film parties by virtue of his marriage to Reynolds, and was certainly not considered a remotely suitable escort for Liz, except of course by her.

As usual there was an element of rebellion in all of this: the more Liz was informed in gossip columns and private advice that Fisher was even less of a good idea than any other man might have been at this time of her life, the more determined she was to exhibit her passion for him. Enraged by the fact that Debbie had not made public the difficulties of her Fisher marriage, Taylor now decided to give an interview to one of her old courtiers, Hedda Hopper, which turned out to be so totally catastrophic as to suggest a complete career death-wish. More probably, in fact, Liz had, as so often, just told the truth as she saw it and then been amazed by the resultant public outcry.

In the course of a long conversation, she gave Hopper one single quote which made appalling banner headlines next day around the known world. Hopper, as she was leaving after what had been a fairly innocuous little chat, casually asked of the Fisher affair, 'And what do you think Mike Todd would have made of all of this?' 'Well,' said Liz, without, one suspects, even the moment's reflection that might have told her to shut up, 'Mike's dead and I'm alive. What do you expect me to do, sleep alone?'

Scandal Time

'If there were ever any doubts
about the ability of Miss Taylor to
express complex and devious
emotions, or to deliver a flexible
and deep performance, *Suddenly
Last Summer* removes all of them'
New York Herald Tribune

$\mathscr{B}$y the end of 1958, Taylor had two major problems: to contain, if at all possible, the damage done by the Hopper interview, and to sort out some sort of a future for herself as a film star and the next Mrs Eddie Fisher. By now her studio was inclined to remain well in the background: long gone were the days when they had rosters of contract stars protected by teams of publicists, and Metro certainly didn't intend to spend what little energy it had left trying to protect an actress who might be anyway about to leave them as most of their others had. Liz was now on her own, and with very few resources: the Todd estate was a financial nightmare that would take years to sort out, with most of his *Around the World* money having apparently disappeared into the film's massive promotion. Fisher meanwhile had just had his television contract cancelled as a penalty for being caught up in a scandalous extramarital affair, and the Reynolds divorce settlement was looming as a large one. They were undoubtedly in a lot of trouble, and can have derived little comfort from checking the precedents: this was just about the time that a survivor of the last great Hollywood extramarital scandal, Ingrid Bergman, was making her return to the American cinema after being exiled for fully eight years for carrying a baby by a man not yet her husband. Taylor wasn't about to spend her next decade in the wilderness, certainly not with three small children and quite possibly also Mr Fisher to support.

Fortunately for her, the moral climate was now changing fast: where Bergman had been literally expelled from American cinemas, nobody any longer could be quite so sure of unified audience reaction. For every cinema-goer shocked and appalled by Taylor's passionate affair with Fisher, there was another who found the whole thing kind of intriguing and sexy and, well, maybe acceptable in a Californian sort of way. Moreover, unlike Bergman, Taylor had her scandal to coincide with a huge box-office hit (*Cat*) rather than a flop (*Joan of Arc*), and that too seemed to condition the general attitude. Metro might now decide, or have, to make do without Taylor, but there was no evidence that Hollywood could: she was suddenly very hot, on screen as well as off. The wife and mother who had been giving some dullish performances in long and worthy epics had overnight become the infinitely more dangerous husband-stealing Maggie the Cat, and there was now an almost tangible aura of excitement around her which had just never been there before.

It was at this traumatic but intriguing time in her career that Taylor finally broke with the studio that had been her home for fifteen years. True, she owed them one more picture, but there was no actual date on that, so in the meantime she went out and found herself an agent, Kurt Frings, and began for the first time to operate independently, making it clear that she was now available to the highest bidder. Frings managed immediately to establish that despite (or perhaps because of) the current scandal, those bids would have to be very high indeed: the first offer that came in, for a film she never made called *Two for the Seesaw*, was already pitched at half a million dollars, and Liz realized that in a bright new world of independent superstardom it would be possible to make more on a single picture than she had acquired in a year or two at Metro. Maybe the future wasn't quite as bleak as Hedda Hopper ('America will never forgive you') had either feared or threatened.

True, there were some minor problems still to overcome: one television studio ordered Liz to stay away during an Eddie Fisher programme because 'the public doesn't like that sort of thing', this presumably being a reference to the affair rather than the actual programme. A group of Cinema Owners withdrew an award they had just given her as 'Star of the Year', but were unable to do anything about the fact that the vastly more prestigious Oscar committee promptly nominated her for her role as Maggie.

Meanwhile, determined to prove that the Fisher affair was going to lead to a serious marriage, Taylor began taking instruction in the Jewish faith and attending all his cabaret performances, though it is not clear which proved the more taxing. By May 1959, Fisher had managed a quickie divorce in Nevada, where he was then working in a nightclub, and Liz had been through her fourth wedding ceremony in nine years, making her now customary vows to retire from the screen and devote herself to the only man who could ever make her truly happy.

The fourth
wedding: to
Eddie Fisher,
May 1959.

The problem with Fisher was that nobody, including
Liz, seems to have been entirely sure what he was there
for. An amiable if not terribly talented pop singer, he was
neither hugely rich like Nicky Hilton, nor elegant and
avuncular like Michael Wilding, nor dynamic like Todd:
he was just kind of there, and usually faintly in the
background as if Liz had lost a suitcase and he'd been told
to be sure and stay behind to locate it. Several observers
reckoned that, as with Todd, an extremely good sexual
relationship was at the root of the marriage, but then
again there were contradictory rumours that Liz, long
before Burton and indeed while still technically on a
Fisher honeymoon, had already gone off for an affair with
Max Lerner, one of the few American press columnists
who had loudly defended her right to remarry so soon
after Todd.

Whatever the reality, Fisher seemed to fulfil the long-felt Taylor need to have a man around the house in some sort of official capacity at all times. Meanwhile the career which had once been her late husband's concern was now in the hands of Kurt Frings, who managed to do a deal with Columbia whereby, as soon as the Fisher wedding had taken place, she would fly to London for *Suddenly Last Summer*. Another steamy Tennessee Williams tale, this one was made over for the screen by Gore Vidal, who saw in it an everyday story of homosexuality and madness and cannibalism. It had started out off-Broadway a year earlier as half of a double-bill called *The Garden District*, and Columbia were now bringing it to the screen with a wealth of talent: Sam Spiegel was the producer, Joseph Mankiewicz the director, Katharine Hepburn the dragon mother who makes her first entrance descending a private elevator demanding 'Are you interested in the Byzantine?' and Taylor as the girl she tries to get lobotomized by Montgomery Clift so that she will not reveal or recall details of how Hepburn's son got unfortunately eaten to death on a North African beach by the boys he was attempting to seduce at the time.

The plot was admittedly not a barrel of laughs, and although this was the film which brought Clift and Taylor together for the third and last time after *Place in the Sun* and *Raintree County*, it was a far from happy set. Taylor was sulking over a hostile reception from the British press,

'Katharine Hepburn is arrestingly mannered, Elizabeth Taylor is courageously whole-hearted, but *Suddenly Last Summer* [1959] remains a Tennessee Williams hothouse fantasy of insanity, homosexuality, mother-domination and cannibalism.'
Sight & Sound

some of whom she had already managed to sue over their comments on the Fisher marriage; Clift was by now deeply into drugs; and Hepburn so disliked her producer and director (both of whom she had happily worked with on such earlier hits as *The African Queen* and *The Philadelphia Story*) that she celebrated the last day of shooting by spitting at them both in the eye, on the grounds that they had treated their cast less than courteously through a difficult time.

Taylor had in fact managed to secure half a million dollars for herself, plus a job for Clift, who was in such bad shape that it was all she could do to stop Spiegel and Mankiewicz replacing him with a young unknown called Peter O'Toole, but she was still not altogether happy with one of the key films that led movie-goers from the still wholesome Fifties into the more permissive Sixties where darker and more sexually explicit subjects were to replace the 'family entertainment' concept that was still at the heart of her old Metro upbringing. Here, as in *Cat*, Taylor established a unique hold on the tortured heroines of Tennessee Williams; more importantly, she also established herself as an unusual combination of romantic movie star and dramatic leading lady, implanting herself firmly on the instant-recall memories of a new generation of film-goers with a classic Columbia ad campaign which had her barely contained within a white low-cut bathing suit while the slogan beneath her ran: 'Suddenly last summer, Cathy knew she was being used for evil'. Up against one of the first ladies of the American screen in Hepburn, Taylor managed to triumph as the wild bird trapped in a terrible kind of despair, and it was largely thanks to her new dramatic superstardom that an uneasy and, many industry insiders thought, possibly uncommercial film managed to make rather more than six million dollars in America alone. Unfortunately for Taylor the Academy, unable to decide between her performance and Hepburn's, nominated them both for Oscars, thereby splitting the film's vote and allowing Simone Signoret to walk away with the statue for *Room at the Top*.

The more the row raged over Liz's fourth marriage, the better she became as an actress and a box-office winner;

she was in fact the last Hollywood star in whose private life press and public took such an obsessive interest, and in the coverage of her Fisher marriage there was already something almost nostalgic and wistful, as if journalists knew they were dealing with the last of the royal clan from a dying country called Hollywood. After Taylor, they would turn to the world of rock music for the great scandals; actresses were allowed to divorce and remarry and steal the occasional husband with vastly less press attention than would still be routinely accorded to Elizabeth, who more than any other movie figure of her time caused a major rethink in newsrooms around America. First of all she declined to sink into the 'doomed superstar' category that had already claimed James Dean and was soon to have Garland and Monroe and Clift among its necrophiliac trophies. Then again, she declined to have her career destroyed by scandal: what had happened to Bergman was patently not happening to her, and from now on she was usually at her most commercially successful in movies when, according to the press, public feeling against her was running at its height. Liz was the first great star to prove that at the height of a marital crisis she had not the faintest need of studio protection, and that too was another of the nails she drove into the coffin of the old Hollywood paternalist contract system of which she had been the last child.

All the same, life as Mrs Fisher was seldom easy: she had only to announce that she had, in deference to Eddie and the late Mike Todd, adopted the Jewish faith for the whole of the Arab League to ban her pictures, an intriguing act of national censorship which meant that hundreds of thousands of Egyptians were later spared the sight of her as their Queen of the Nile in *Cleopatra*. Moreover, although her new-found strength in good movies was enough to ride through the storm of public protest at her marriage to Fisher, his career was not in such good shape and took a considerable beating. His ex-wife Debbie Reynolds was still giving tearful press interviews about being abandoned, and it soon became clear that Eddie's best hope of a future lay in promoting his new wife rather than continuing to slog around the nightclub circuit, to which new end he solemnly announced to an aghast

London press that he would shortly be producing Liz as *Anna Karenina*. Somehow, and very unfairly, Fisher became the fall-guy in the tale of Taylor's marriages and his name soon became a shorthand note of what not to do when your husband gets killed. 'The public will never turn against me,' said Mrs John F. Kennedy a few years into her widowhood, 'unless of course I marry Eddie Fisher.'

In fact it was Fisher who held together his new wife in her continuing grief over Todd, a man he too had deeply loved, and who gave her young children yet another father figure; his problem was that like her first two husbands he lacked the sheer force of character to make their marriage anything like the equal partnership that she had enjoyed with her last husband. For a while life worked out well enough, however, and Taylor made regular appearances at stage-side tables during his cabaret routines. She also, in a constant determination to drum up trade for close relatives, made a guest appearance in a memorable

Cinerama disaster called *Holiday in Spain* and produced by her stepson Michael Todd Jr, with whom she had occasionally been seen out on the town after his father's death. Viewers of this desperately unexciting mystery thriller were more than a little confused by lingering shots of characters lighting pipes or sniffing bunches of flowers, until it was explained that the film was originally entitled *Scent of Mystery* and the intention had been to spray its audiences with whiffs of tobacco or flower perfume at the appropriate moment. Unfortunately this pioneering contribution to cine-history was defeated by the fact that few theatre managers had the faintest idea how to work the device which would fill their halls with the correct whiff at the right dramatic moment, and as a result the movie never quite achieved the sweet smell of success, becoming instead one of the great turkeys of the year and taking away with it a considerable part of the Todd fortune that Liz might have hoped would be hers. Mercifully she did, however, still own the copyright in the title song of *Around the World in Eighty Days*, which had been one of Todd's final and more intelligent gifts to her.

It was while she was in London working on the film of *Suddenly Last Summer*, one night in the middle of 1959, that the phone rang in her hotel suite at the Dorchester. This time it was not her current director Joe Mankiewicz ('She is close to being the greatest actress in the world and has done it all by instinct; she is still a primitive, the Grandma Moses of acting') but another distinguished Hollywood figure, Walter Wanger, with an intriguing suggestion for 1960. Spyros Skouras at Fox had commissioned him to produce a remake of *Cleopatra* and a list of possible stars had been compiled which ranged somewhat wildly from Joan Collins and Dana Wynter through Susan Hayward and Marilyn Monroe to Brigitte Bardot, Jennifer Jones, Kim Novak, Audrey Hepburn, Sophia Loren and Gina Lollobrigida. Eventually, and very uneasily, Skouras and Wanger came to the same conclusion: only one actress working in 1959 commanded the right kind of public fascination for *Cleopatra* and she was Elizabeth Taylor. Hence the phone call, which Liz took with a certain detached amusement, thinking, and perhaps rightly in view of what later transpired, that the whole idea of a *Cleopatra* remake was singularly unpromising. This was however a time of wide-screen epics, and Wanger was already so desperate for a star that when Taylor said she would do it for a million dollars against ten per cent of the gross, plus script and location approval, to her considerable amazement he agreed.

But they had reckoned without MGM, to whom she still owed one final picture on the fifteen-year contract. Metro had been lying low during the early months of the Fisher marriage, not wishing to associate themselves with a scandalous contract player until it had been safely established that she could still sell tickets around the country. This became clear on both *Cat* and *Suddenly Last Summer*: denied an actual Oscar on both nominations, she had nonetheless turned both films into major box-office winners and the studio was keen to cash in on her for one last time, moreover at an agreed rate of $120,000, barely more than a tenth of what she could be getting for *Cleopatra*.

MGM at last had their most recalcitrant daughter over a barrel: unless she agreed to give them one last picture, with a script of their choosing, they would tie her up legally in such a way that she would never get to do *Cleopatra*. Accordingly, and with a very bad grace indeed, she agreed to give them *Butterfield 8*, John O'Hara's story of a New York call girl whose unhappy affair with a married man leads to her death in a car crash. The studio had owned the property since it first appeared in 1935 as a

'Here we have the ancient, hackneyed story of the tinseled but tarnished prostitute. '
New York Times

METRO-GOLDWYN-MAYER PRESENTS
ELIZABETH TAYLOR
LAURENCE HARVEY
EDDIE FISHER

IN JOHN O'HARA'S **BUTTERFIELD 8**

co-starring DINA MERRILL
with MILDRED DUNNOCK · BETTY FIELD
JEFFREY LYNN · KAY MEDFORD · SUSAN OLIVER
Screen Play by CHARLES SCHNEE and JOHN MICHAEL HAYES
in CinemaScope and Metrocolor · Directed by DANIEL MANN
A PANDRO S. BERMAN PRODUCTION

'Miss Taylor tries very hard to get a tragic quality into the girl, but not even acting can help *Butterfield 8.*' *Saturday Review*

novel built around the true story of Starr Faithfull, and having waited that long to see his work on screen, Mr O'Hara was understandably less than delighted to hear Taylor at regular press conferences denounce the story as sleazy and pornographic. She was doing it, she announced, purely as a contractual obligation, though she did insist on having Fisher play her sympathetic buddy in a performance which managed quite remarkably to be even more woodenly miscast than that of Laurence Harvey as the wealthy married socialite who drives her to her doom. 'Glossy balderdash,' thought Alexander Walker, while John O'Hara later acknowledged: 'The cracks Miss Taylor has taken at my novel gave me some bruises which were healed by the MGM accounting department with their tender, loving royalty cheques.' Critics generally were appalled by the way that O'Hara's originally very touching tragedy of a tart had been turned into a sleek soap-opera, and the final irony was that it was here, rather than in *Cat* or *Suddenly Last Summer*, that Taylor was finally to win her long-awaited Oscar, though not before she had undergone yet another crisis operation.

What had happened was that after the filming of *Butterfield 8* ('The number you have dialled,' noted the *Newsweek* critic wittily, 'is not a working number') she and Eddie had gone for a cruise around the Greek islands and then returned to London to start on the already long-delayed *Cleopatra*, for which Peter Finch and Stephen Boyd had also been contracted as Caesar and Mark Antony. At Pinewood Studios, eight and a half acres had been turned over to the rebuilding of ancient Egypt at a cost already approaching another million of the dollars that had been promised to Taylor. Technicians were talking direly of the last *Cleopatra* fiasco, one with Vivien Leigh in the middle 1940s which had virtually bankrupted Gabriel Pascal, and somebody seemed to have forgotten about traditional English weather. By the time shooting started in September 1960 it was already raining, and by the time they got to the first big crowd scene in October several hundred extras got lost in fog. Taylor had by now developed a nasty cold, and nobody seemed to have done anything very much about a script: three years later, when the film was finally released, this was credited to its eventual director Joseph Mankiewicz plus 'Ranald MacDougall, Sidney Buchman, Plutarch, Suetonius, Appian and C. M. Franzero', though not all of those were around at the time to claim their percentage.

Day by expensive day, *Cleopatra* was overtaking even the Vivien Leigh version to become the most costly fiasco seen in a British studio since the abortive filming of the Charles Laughton *I Claudius* back in 1936. Writers were summoned almost daily from California, Taylor retired to the London Clinic with meningitis, and eventually Wanger decided to cut his already marathon losses and shut the production down until the beginning of 1961, by which time the rain might have stopped, or Taylor's health might have improved, or some other miracle could have come along. Already however the film that was supposed to save Fox (theirs had been the original Hollywood version with Theda Bara back in 1917) was looking very like the film that was going to put the final nail into an already mortally ill studio's coffin. But there was no going back, and no going ahead without Taylor who was

The Oscar committee thought otherwise: with Yul Brynner, receiving her *Butterfield 8* Academy Award.

by now deeply embedded in the epic package. Who else could claim a late-1950s consecutive trio of major box-office risks turned around into smash commercial hits by sheer force of personal stardom, while still being able to look back on a movie-making career of thirty films in seventeen years, not one of which had ever lost real money?

So it had to be Taylor, though directors, like writers and co-stars, proved expendable: by the time they were ready to resume shooting, the original pilot of the film Rouben Mamoulian was off the picture, replaced (many said at Liz's insistence) by Joseph L. Mankiewicz, who had guided her safely through *Suddenly Last Summer* and promised now to do something drastic about the script as well as a budget that, with all the delays, was already dangerously out of hand.

During the lay-off Liz occupied herself with major lawsuits against a couple of London papers which had claimed that she was either too fat or too drugged for *Cleopatra* to roll, and it took several years before the truth finally dawned that not all the epic problems of the movie could be laid at the door of her hotel suite. To go into a multi-million dollar historical saga with no real script, and only the haziest notion of how the burning Roman sun could be conjured up through an English winter fog, was asking for trouble on a level that even Taylor couldn't deliver alone.

By the time they resumed work at Pinewood in February it did begin to look as if there were going to be a picture after all: Mankiewicz was costing at least another million dollars, since he had to be bought out of various other projects, but he had managed to bring Lawrence Durrell on to the script (Nunnally Johnson and Paddy Chayevsky having both reckoned it unwritable in the wake of Shakespeare and Shaw), and Taylor was no longer begging for her release. The plan now was to abandon most of what little had already been shot and go again with the new writer-director team, a plan which might even have worked had it not been for a new catastrophe which befell the project on 4 March, when Taylor, having apparently recovered from all her previous winter ailments, was rushed into the London Clinic with lung congestion so severe that it threatened to cut off her oxygen supply and choke her to death. Whatever press and public cynicism there had been about some of her previous hospital crises, there was no lack of evidence that on this occasion she was, for a while, as close to death as made very little difference. The Queen's doctor was summoned, crowds formed outside the Clinic, and headlines around the world reported hourly bulletins detailing a slow recovery during which another major change of tide could be sensed in public perception of Taylor. No longer a thoroughly tiresome, much-married, husband-stealing Hollywood movie star being paid a million dollars for failing to make a picture, she had now and over a few days become a gallant fighter for her own life who had been to death's door and returned to tell attentive journalists the tale.

This clearly appalling and frightening time had two immediate effects: it put Taylor virtually in sole charge of *Cleopatra*, since she could now dictate the terms on which she would return to a project which still did not exist without her, and it took her straight back into the embrace of the Californian establishment to whom she flew immediately on checking out of the London Clinic. This was not another of the self-induced illnesses of a Garland or a Monroe in psychological distress: here were venerable men who had attended monarchs talking of tracheotomies and a miracle survival. If James Dean's early death in a car crash had been, in the words of one cynic at least, a good career move, then this medical catastrophe not only nearly killed Taylor but also saved her in public estimation simply because there was no doubting its reality. Liz herself later recalled in gruesome detail how they had to 'slit open my throat and stick a pump down it to take all the stuff out of my lungs', and not surprisingly she took the view that she was about to die.

When she didn't, and moreover recovered sufficiently to get herself and the children and Fisher back to California for the Oscar ceremony in mid-April, it was like a regal homecoming. For the last four consecutive years (*Raintree County, Cat, Suddenly Last Summer* and now *Butterfield 8*) she had been nominated for an Academy Award without as yet getting anywhere near an actual statue. This time things were different. Although nobody in their right critical mind could claim that of those four performances *Butterfield 8* had been the best, and there were many who would argue that it was by some distance the worst of the quartet, the climate around Los Angeles had now altered drastically in Liz's favour: the last surviving superstar, the only one to enter the 1960s with a million-dollar contract already signed, had come back to them from the valley of the shadow of death, and if that wasn't worth an award then what on earth was?

Thus it was that Gloria Wandrous, John O'Hara's 'slut of all time', the role that Taylor herself said was the worst assignment of her entire career, a 'sick nymphomaniac' and an insult to American womanhood, wound up beating Melina Mercouri, Deborah Kerr, Greer Garson and the much-fancied (for *The Apartment*) Shirley MacLaine to win Elizabeth Taylor her first-ever Oscar. Seldom can sheer sentiment, even in Hollywood, have had such a victory; even Debbie Reynolds acknowledged that she had voted for Taylor in relief at her medical survival, and it was left to Shirley MacLaine to get the whole event into

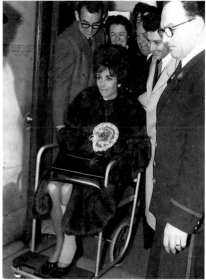

some kind of cheerful perspective. 'I lost that Oscar,' she noted later, 'to a tracheotomy.'

With Liz restored to public favour, and her husband also seen in a more kindly light for having stood so long by her hospital bed, it began to look as though even *Cleopatra* might be retrieved from the abyss. True, the original London cast had now dispersed to other jobs, with audible sighs of relief from both Peter Finch and Stephen Boyd that they had escaped after very nearly a year of standby non-shooting from what threatened to be a life's work, but that left Mankiewicz free to rebuild the film in his own rather academic image. The Pinewood sets were written off to tax, new designs were ordered, and a whole new schedule was drawn up for shooting to start in Rome, which had certain natural advantages for a story largely concerned with Julius Caesar and Mark Antony, towards the end of September.

In the meantime Taylor attended a film festival in Moscow, where she threatened locals with her remake of *Anna Karenina*, and began for the first time to enjoy a kind of press and public attention which had suddenly grown respectful rather than prurient. At a time when most other great stars seemed to be disappearing into road crashes or drug clinics or just old age, Taylor was still only on the verge of her thirtieth birthday but could already be billed as one of the few great survivors, in movies as in remarriages and medical history. What was more, she now held an Oscar to validate that survival in the only

Clinical traumas: in and out of the London Clinic with Eddie Fisher in 1960.

language Californians really spoke; 1961 was the one year of her lifelong career that she ever spent at the top of box-office popularity charts all over America.

Journalists now wrote respectfully if repetitively of her 'fight for survival', often leaving it tactfully unclear whether they were referring to victories over tracheotomies, divorce laws, public opinion, studio moguls or just scripts as shaky as *Butterfield 8*. Ironically and teeth-grindingly, Metro had finally said farewell to their contract star of seventeen years at the one moment when she might have been able to do them a bit of good, especially as in the lady herself there was evidence of a new kind of enthusiasm and dedication. With Fisher relegated to the role of manager and potential producer (it

With Eddie Fisher and producer Walter Wanger on the set of *Cleopatra* (1963).

was announced that she would in future only work for his production company, though in the event she never did), and the children settled in various schools, Liz suddenly found herself able to think about a career that almost began to seem worth pursuing:

'I've been acting for nineteen years now, and from the first it came very easily, like playing games, which is maybe why I always found it so boring, just a kind of hobby and then later a chore. For a while, when I was married to Mike Todd whose wedding ring I still wear as well as Eddie's, I really did want to give up the whole thing forever, but lately I've been thinking that maybe I do want to be an actress after all. Off screen I'm still shy, lazy, unpunctual and sloppy, with a major vice about eating whenever possible; but after being so desperately ill I've decided that there are some roles I actually want to live to play, and Cleopatra is one of them. It will be a lot of fun being the first Jewish Queen of Egypt.'

First, however, there had to be a Caesar and a Mark Antony, and yet another attempt to get her off-screen life into some sort of order. Up front the Fisher marriage was apparently all right, but privately it was already doomed: failing to find in a genially nondescript crooner the kind of dynamic impresario of her life that had been evident in Todd or even the father-figure of Wilding, she had gone back to the Max Lerner affair and was also to be found from time to time with Richard Brooks. No longer able to have the children whom she always thought the only real validation of a marriage, she and Fisher tried to adopt one or two, including those she had already had by Michael Wilding; when the English actor understandably lodged a mild objection to this plan, she scooped up her Wilding and Todd children plus Fisher and moved them all to Rome for what was clearly going to be a long siege. Rex Harrison had by now been cast to play Julius Caesar; for Mark Antony, Wanger and Mankiewicz eventually settled on a 35-year-old Welsh actor with a distinguished classical record in the British theatre but a hitherto very lacklustre Hollywood life. However, he had just taken Broadway by storm as the romantic King Arthur in Lerner and Loewe's musical of *Camelot*, and his name was Richard Burton.

Serpent of the Nile

'When I was with him on the set of *Cleopatra* I fell in love with him and I have loved him ever since, practically my whole adult life'

'*S*leeping with Elizabeth,' Richard Burton once told me with disarming modesty several years into what had become the most notorious and heavily world-publicized alliance since the Duke of Windsor ran off with another two-time divorcee from the United States, 'put my price up from a quarter to half a million dollars a picture, but I really didn't do it on purpose; how was I to know that she was the most famous fucking woman in the world?'

Curiously enough, he could just about have been telling the truth; even in those days, it took a dedicated follower of Hollywood newsprint to detect all the complex seismic shifts in Taylor's public image, and global interest in her had really only begun with the Fisher scandal and then the life-or-death tracheotomy of a few months earlier. It is therefore possible that Burton, deeply involved in London with the Old Vic through the late 1950s and then for more than a year with the Broadway creation and run of *Camelot*, arrived in Rome still vaguely thinking of his new co-star as Todd's widow or the third party in a rather nasty divorce, rather than as the now universal superstar whom only Jackie Kennedy would shift out of the headlines, and even then not until she too had been widowed and moved rather too quickly into a widely unpopular subsequent marriage.

Like Rex Harrison, but unlike almost all of Taylor's previous California co-stars, Burton came of a strictly 'legit' theatre background and took an amiably dim view of the movies. Where to Liz they were still the only way of life she had ever known, no matter how often she had tried to find another, to Rex and Richard they (and especially the huge-budget *Cleopatra*) were merely a useful way of making relatively quick money between more demanding and honourable but modestly paid stage engagements. Both men were therefore more than a little amazed, in venturing on to what was unquestionably Taylor's Roman territory, by their first experience of her awesome stardom and distinctly untheatrical working methods.

Essentially the difference was that they were expensively hired hands while she was by now the alibi for the entire project: 'If Taylor coughs,' as one of the Italian actors on the set put it, 'Fox catches pneumonia.' Through

all the traumas of the past year it had become painfully apparent that she alone could sell this giant at the box-office, and her word was therefore law. Not that she was often unprofessional in the sense of a Garland or a Monroe during their brief periods of box-office power; the old Metro training from childhood still ran too deep for that, and she was usually the first on the set each morning, which was just as well since it took her and several trained artists a couple of hours to get into that remarkable eye make-up. But she still found rehearsing an obscure stage tradition, and therefore did very little until the cameras were actually rolling, by which time Harrison and Burton had usually come to the mistaken conclusion that she wasn't going to do anything at all and that they should tone their own performances down accordingly. As the cameras rolled she would then characteristically come to life, and steal those few scenes where the theft amounted to anything more worthwhile than petty larceny.

Because of the abortive and rain-soaked English start, the long lay-off, and then the cost of relocating the whole extravaganza at Cinecittà, *Cleopatra* was already tens of millions of dollars over budget and at least one other entire picture (a Pinewood farce called *Carry on Cleo*) was to be made on its discarded sets. On those mornings when Taylor was a little late, therefore, Mankiewicz was not about to complain too loudly; a late Taylor was still better than no Taylor at all, there were remarkably few scenes that could be shot around her, and if she could just be kept happy and reasonably thin and preferably far from any hospital for the duration, then they might even manage to finish up with a film in the can, which is largely why Eddie Fisher was retained on a substantial salary, with his own office staff, to be her principal minder.

And the epic confusions of *Cleopatra* were indeed very seldom of her making: the Italian film industry knew a gift from heaven when it saw one coming over the Atlantic, and the Hollywood unit was duly ripped off in every department, from costumes (which were quite literally ripped, thereby necessitating several expensive weeks of local remaking) to the teams of extras who turned up only when collecting sizeable paychecks and seemed never to have come across any kind of a toga.

Typical of this confusion was that Burton had been contracted (and expensively bought out of the New York run of *Camelot*) to start work at the same time as Harrison, apparently by someone back in California who had failed to notice that it would take approximately seventeen weeks of daily shooting to cover all the Harrison scenes that had to elapse before Caesar met his death in the Capitol and Burton could formally enter the action for the epic's second half.

That left Burton with an awful lot of time to sit on the sidelines of the set, and though he had a few friends around (notably such stalwart old Welsh allies as Rachel Roberts, who was soon to marry Harrison, and Stanley Baker, who was also filming then at Cinecittà), what

'The tedium of *Cleopatra* is only occasionally lightened by the laughable vulgarity of its display.' *New Republic*

Richard principally did was to stare in some fascination at Elizabeth. He had worked with many better and more classically trained actresses before, and even a few old-style California stars; indeed his first Hollywood assignment back in 1951 had been *My Cousin Rachel* opposite Olivia de Havilland; but he had never come across an alliance of stardom and sexuality in quite such high definition as was then apparent in Taylor; nor had he ever met anyone who was so totally and utterly the creation and creature of film.

Clearly he had to have an affair with her, but there was nothing so very unusual in that. A loving and tolerant first wife, Sybil, had watched him having affairs with several leading ladies and some very minor players as well without doing much damage to a very settled domestic life; and recently most of the cast of *Camelot* (whose favourite backstage song had become the slightly rewritten Lerner and Loewe classic 'I Wonder Who the King Is Screwing Tonight') had seen him off to Rome warning him only not to get too deeply involved with Liz. No one ever told him not to get involved with her at all, and from the time they eventually got around to shooting their first lethargic love scenes it was patently clear that they had already fallen deeply for each other.

What nobody seems to have bargained for at all, and certainly not the two principals, was the hothouse element whereby their occasional late-night suppers at Alfredo's would reach the headlines almost before the fettucine was served in a city which had just invented the paparazzi. *Cleopatra* was already, because the most expensively delayed, the most closely watched of movies in progress; rumours that the Taylor marriage was rocky had been all over town for weeks, as had stories of Burton's regular romantic interest in co-stars, and by the time they started their affair they were thus already following a script that could have been drawn up by a team of desperate local hacks.

At the time they began working together, almost half-way into the film's long shooting schedule, almost everyone knew there was something between them, though nobody could be entirely sure quite what, not even the director who told his aghast producer finally that he

had been sitting on a volcano for too long and that 'Richard and Liz are not just playing Antony and Cleopatra'. There would be some critics who later reckoned that they were in fact hardly playing them at all, but that was not the problem. The problem was essentially that, now as always, whenever Liz fell in love it seemed logical to her that she should then get married to the object of her new affections. The logic of this was never clear to Burton, who still had a perfectly good wife and children set up in a villa across town, nor to Fisher, who could hardly bring himself to believe that after all the agony they had so recently gone through in getting married, the whole doomed liaison was to be so speedily unscrambled.

For a while, even Liz seemed to accept the impossibility of yet another marital break-up – this would be her third divorce and, if organized, fifth marriage in rather less than twelve years. Clinging briefly to Eddie, she therefore announced that despite scandalous Roman rumour the marriage was just fine and they would be adopting a little girl, Maria, since she could not herself have another baby. For a week or two that ended press speculation and even Burton seemed relieved: maybe he could now get on with his own marriage and the Taylor affair under normal extramarital conditions.

Then, in Rex Harrison's recollection, 'the balloon went up'. Fisher, his pride understandably hurt by the unmistakability of Taylor's passion for Burton, decided to push it to a confrontation. Burton, still deeply uncertain that an affair was worth the destruction of two marriages, retreated to his wife, at which point Liz retreated as usual to hospital where this time, it being a Roman hospital almost eager to stay in the headlines that she brought to it, the rumours were of everything from a suicide attempt to a stomach upset.

By now *Cleopatra* had become a kind of black farce in which everything mattered but the actual filming itself, despite Harrison's increasingly tetchy pleas from the sidelines for everyone to try and maintain a little professional dignity and theatrical or at least cinematic discipline. But matters were way beyond that: when Spyros Skouras, the head of Fox, was summoned to Rome to salvage or at least try to protect his studio's considerable investment, his airport quote for the hordes of assembled journalists was 'It's all rubbish,' though whether he was referring to yet another amended screenplay, the reports of a Burton romance, or those of a Taylor suicide attempt, he never had the chance to make clear.

Meanwhile it was obvious to everyone that, marriages or no marriages, the one thing no one could live with was Taylor in hospital, since there were still precious few shots in the movie that could be achieved without her and most of those were battle sequences to be filmed far from Cinecittà at the very end of the everlasting schedule. Both Burton and Taylor therefore reappeared in the studio, and work continued until the morning of her thirtieth birthday, 27 February 1962, when she was reported to be 'very disturbed' by the landmark anniversary and not much cheered by a large diamond ring from Fisher. By now Burton had taken to accosting Eddie at parties off the set and telling him how much he loved his wife, whereupon Fisher decided that absence might make the heart grow fonder; either that or he was as keen as most others to get as far away from the tortured *Cleopatra* set as possible, since morale there had sunk to an all-time low with the

'If you want to devote the best part of four hours to looking at Elizabeth Taylor in all her draped and undraped physical splendour, then this is your movie; in royal regalia, en negligee or au naturel, she gives the impression that she is at one of Miami Beach's more exotic resorts.' *New York Herald Tribune*

realization that there were still several more months of dialogue to go and that the only public interest now centred on what Antony and Cleopatra were getting up to in their dressing-rooms.

Accordingly Fisher flew to New York in mid-March, and was there persuaded to give a press conference denying all rumours that his marriage was in trouble and that Liz had left him for Burton. That denial might just have held for a few more weeks, had Fisher not decided to impress the assembled hacks by placing an international phone call to Taylor on the set in Rome, during which he asked her to deny that there was any kind of a problem. 'Well, Eddie,' said Liz over the phone, in the hearing of several dozen pressmen, exhibiting nothing more than her usual dazzling honesty in a crisis, 'I can't actually do that because there is, you see, some truth in the rumours.'

So that was more or less that: Fisher now decided that his turn had come to retire to hospital; Sybil Burton went into understandable shock, not so much at her husband's infidelity as the way in which on this occasion the stakes had been raised to global and divorce proportions; the adoption agency began to wonder what they were doing handing over Maria to Liz; and the prime movers of the crisis occupied themselves with a film which was beginning to seem more and more irrelevant to all but its embattled and weary makers.

Reckoning they had nothing more to lose, Richard and Liz began to be seen on the nightclub circuit, to the delight of the paparazzi. All casting had now been altered so that Fisher (only recently the villain who had broken up a Debbie Reynolds marriage) thus became a prime source of sympathy, with Liz back as the temptress and Burton as a likely Welsh lad on the make. Trade papers took the view that 20th Century Fox were getting a raw deal from their stars, though the publicity was now greater than that attending any other film in the entire history of cinema, while the Vatican, presumably incensed that the whole ghastly affair was unrolling by their own back door, denounced Taylor's behaviour as that of 'an intemperate vamp who destroys families and devours husbands'. Art Buchwald, noting that the affair had driven talk of nuclear disarmament and a Berlin settlement right off the front pages of the world's press, reckoned that there should be some kind of national referendum on what Liz should do now, with those who abstained being held to have shirked their moral duty and lost all right to interfere in her life ever again. *Photoplay* obliged by actually running such a poll to discover whether its readers 'could ever forgive what Liz has done'. Some could, it seemed, and some could not. Meanwhile the Vatican had taken to accusing her of 'erotic vagrancy' and being an unfit mother.

Looking at all that press coverage a quarter of a century later, it is hard to understand quite what was being fought out over the columns. Other film stars had run off with each other or each other's husbands and wives, and were indeed to go on doing so for the foreseeable future. But in the Taylor coverage there was a kind of international hysteria, as though journalists had realized that this was the end of that particular era, that never again would

'Miss Taylor plays Cleopatra as a plump young American matron in a number of Egyptian costumes and make-ups.' *New Republic*

there be a star quite as easily able to occupy the world's headlines for days if not weeks at a time. Just as *Cleopatra* was, because of its still spiralling costs, already being written off as the last of the multi-million-dollar epics, even though in fact it was to inspire a handful of others, before the whole genre disappeared into the tighter budgeting of the 1970s, so this was quite evidently also going to be the last of the great Hollywood expatriate scandals before the industry fragmented into television, and all those involved seemed to feel that they had better make the most of it. Books were written, magazine serials commissioned, tele-documentaries set up, all ostensibly about the making of *Cleopatra* but all in fact about the mating of Liz and Richard, two actors who just happened to be playing the world's best-known lovers in the world's most expensive movie, thereby capturing a stranglehold on the world's gossip columns in a manner only fleetingly achieved five years earlier by Taylor's old Metro rival Grace Kelly when she had married the last of the world's fairytale princes.

Somewhat amazed to find that an affair he had started out of Roman boredom and superstar curiosity had now become an issue of world importance, Burton began discreetly to panic. Taylor had after all already been through two husbands who were, at least in a remote sense, actors; and both Michael Wilding and Eddie Fisher had ended their marriages to her as nervous wrecks, with their own careers in ruins. It was not a fate that much appealed to Burton, least of all because unlike the others he had started out with a career worth preserving in its own right. Moreover, though he was undoubtedly much in love with Liz, his own marriage was still a lot stronger than those of any of Taylor's previous husbands-of-others. Then again, she was still in the throes of an adoption, and he had young daughters to support; maybe the Vatican was right and marriage wasn't such a good idea after all.

On the other hand, they and the world press had now come so far down that path it might be easier to go on than turn back; if they were already the extramarital villains of the universe, there wasn't a lot more harm any publicity could do them. Besides which, attitudes were on the turn: despite press hysteria, nobody in 1962 was any longer absolutely certain that their moral turpitude was a hanging issue, and a kind of black jokiness was already emerging from the situation: 'If you really want the truth,' Joe Mankiewicz told a desperate newshound, 'it is that Richard and I are deeply in love and Liz is the cover for our affair.' That kind of joke might not have worked on Hedda Hopper or Louella Parsons back in California and anyway at the end of their long reigns, but in the European Sixties there were indications that for every cinema-goer aghast at the immorality of Richard and Liz, there was another who rather liked and maybe even envied their romantic courage in cutting through all other legal and matrimonial obligations in order to reach each other. Wasn't that the way lovers were supposed to behave? If not, what was *Cleopatra* all about anyway?

As shooting of its second half ground on into the

summer, events off camera continued to be of more interest than anything happening under the arc lights. Taylor announced that she was divorcing Fisher just as soon as either of them could get to Nevada; Burton announced that he was returning to his wife; Taylor thereupon re-entered hospital (rumours this time ranged from a car crash to an urgent stomach-pumping); and somewhere in all of that they found time to finish the movie that several of its participants were now regarding as more of an occupational hazard than a job. It was, invariably, Burton who gave the best interviews ('Show a Welshman a thousand doors, of which one is marked Self-Destruction, and that he will take'), but Taylor who still brought down on her own head the wrath of middle America. Denounced from its pulpits, derided on its chat shows, deplored by its gossip columnists, she yet remained the only real story in showbusiness, and now that *Cleopatra* was about to wrap at an estimated total print cost of just over $37,000,000 there was a kind of uneasiness about what everyone would do next. Clearly 20th Century Fox would never be the same again, indeed most of the executives at the sharp end had already been replaced a couple of times during the nightmare shooting, but there were journalists with whole careers built around that one hilarious year in Rome. If everybody now dispersed, whole fan magazines could be in trouble for other stories: movies like *Cleopatra* just didn't happen any more anywhere else in the world.

Paparazzi attention therefore soon switched from Italy to Switzerland, where both Richard and Elizabeth had chalets, his a modest affair at Celigny and hers a rather more lavish Todd-endowed structure near Gstaad. They spent much of the summer in isolation a few miles apart, periodically announcing to the ever-watchful press that they were certainly not planning to meet, and were indeed heavily engaged on trying to put their own marriages and families back together again after the Roman follies and what had been a difficult, not to say hysterical, year for all concerned. Burton was talking seriously to any journalist who'd listen about the importance of returning to life with Sybil; Liz talked merely about bringing up the Wilding and Todd children as well as the newly adopted Maria, having apparently accepted that the Fisher marriage was all over, regardless of whatever happened with Burton.

What happened was that by August they had begun to meet again in Geneva, Switzerland being a remarkably small country, and by September it was evident even to them, let alone a delighted press, that all other alliances were now over and they would therefore continue to co-star, if no longer in *Cleopatra* then in an ongoing daily soap opera called *The Burtons* which was to carry them through two marriages to each other, two divorces (quite apart from the ones they had to get from previous partners), ten films, a television series and a catastrophic Broadway stage season only a few months before his sudden death in 1984, by which time they had been publicly locked together even during subsequent marriages as, for almost a quarter of a century, the most famous movie couple in the whole history of world cinema.

Surprisingly, none of this did a lot of good to *Cleopatra*: the everlasting epic was now to be locked up in a cutting-room for almost another year while sundry producers, directors and studio chiefs fought (and usually lost their jobs) over its final screen shape. Meanwhile, it did not take rival studios long to reach an obvious conclusion: if

'The producers may not have extended the frontiers of cinema, but they have completed under harrowing conditions a respectable job of spectacle-making.' *Variety*

Burton and Taylor were now the hottest properties in the box-office world, and if the film that had brought them together was so gargantuan that it could not be shown for twelve months – and even then to appalling reviews if the word of mouth from the location was anything to go by – surely a production company which could get its stars into the cinemas quickly enough, and with altogether an easier movie for audiences and makers alike, would then be looking at several million dollars in quick profit. It would be the ultimate steal from 20th Century Fox of their one surviving crown jewel, and there was a certain ironic delight at Taylor's old MGM studio that they should be the ones to organize the heist.

What Metro knew was that Burton, eager to continue a movie career which had been tied up for a year in *Cleopatra*, and feeling that whether or not he went for the divorce he still needed some quick money, had agreed to go to work for them on *The VIPs*, an omnibus tale of airline passengers grounded by a heavy fog at Heathrow which in some way would alter all their separate lives. Based clearly on the model of *Grand Hotel*, and the forerunner of *The Yellow Rolls Royce*, which came from the same author and director, *The VIPs* had actually begun with its writer Terence Rattigan hearing of a moment in his friend Vivien Leigh's tortured life when she was attempting to run away from Laurence Olivier with Peter Finch, only to find herself for several hours staring out into London Airport fog. The idea intrigued Rattigan and his director Anthony Asquith, who both had a taste for stylish, well-made romantic movies of the old school, and a remarkable supporting cast of fellow travellers was assembled, including Orson Welles, Maggie Smith, Louis Jourdan, Elsa Martinelli and Margaret Rutherford; while way down the cast-list in fleeting appearances could be found Alan Howard, Richard Briers and David Frost.

Burton was playing the millionaire industrialist whose wife was attempting to fly away from him with playboy Louis Jourdan, and the first idea had been that Sophia Loren should play the woman; but when Burton and Taylor came together again, she agreed to take on the role. MGM knew at once what they had got: the instructions were to have nobody talk to anybody, to get the film in the

End of an epic.

can as quickly as was humanly possible and on a relatively tight budget (though Liz was still getting her now usual million dollars) and to have it out on release before anyone had a chance to forget about the world's most famous lovers.

And it worked: *The VIPs* may not be another *Grand Hotel* but it doesn't fall that far short of it, while to have Liz up there on the screen agonizing over whether to leave her husband (in this case Burton) for her lover meant that the movie could go into profit within days of its first release. In that sense, *The VIPs* was the first of the true Burton-Taylor films, and it established an extraordinary precedent: for the next five years, until the whole double-act came crashing down suitably enough with *Dr Faustus*, every film they made, whether together or apart, good, bad or indifferent, took tens of millions of dollars at the box-office. Even *Cleopatra* did that, though unfortunately not as many tens of millions as it had cost to make, only breaking even after an eventual resale deal to television. Such had been the intensity of the Rome affair, known to its participants and bystanders forever afterwards as *le scandale*, that it guaranteed the Burtons fully five years of immunity from poor reviews or bad scripts or appalling performances. Theirs were the last of the films to which audiences around the world went simply because they were in them, regardless of plot or other artistic considerations.

Back at Fox, however, a new *Cleopatra* problem arose: how were they to sell the troubled giant if its stars were already on at half the other cinemas in town with a quite different and rather more accessible picture? One solution appeared quickly enough in Times Square: a billboard, several hundred feet square, showing just the two of them against a background of the Nile. But no sooner had it been built high above Broadway than Rex Harrison's lawyers were on the phone to Fox: their client had an 'equality of billing' clause somewhere deep in his contract and would also have to appear on the poster, thereby making the 'world's greatest lovers' into something of a *menage à trois*. By this time even Liz could see the hilarity of the whole doomed enterprise. What they really should show on the poster, she thought, were the film's writer and

With Richard
Burton and
Louis Jourdan
as *The VIPS*
(1963).

director and producer and maybe Sigmund Freud as well.
Appalled by the dismissal of Mankiewicz during the film's
editing, thoroughly uneasy over advance reports from
industry friends about how bad the four-hour saga actually was, Taylor and Burton now began talking about it as
if they could head off the really bad reviews by issuing
worse ones themselves. Taylor at least had been living
with the project on and off for the best part of about five
years: she had been one of the first to recognize the trouble
they were in with a story which had already been done
more or less definitively by Shakespeare and Shaw and
Claudette Colbert, and the first to beg them to get in some
kind of recognizable writers. For Burton it had been just
another costume picture; for Taylor, it was something
rather more, the first film since her Oscar and the one
which she had to carry from its opening sequences to its
credit titles. A failure for *Cleopatra* would be a failure for
her, far more than for any of its other participants, and
her bitterness at the chaos on the set (albeit partially of
her own making) and now in the cutting-rooms was
beginning to become only too evident in the press.

Indeed, soon after the film was first released, to some

Mr and Mrs Richard Burton at the races: Sandown Park 1964.

hysterically bad reviews and a few polite public yawns, Fox filed a massive breach-of-contract suit asking for fifty million dollars from Richard and Elizabeth in recognition of the 'damage' they had caused their own film on every level. Few fully understood, noted Art Buchwald acidly, that when the studio claimed the film would make a hundred million dollars they intended to earn half that by suing its stars. The Fox case was complex and eventually settled out of court, but essentially it was based on the notion that Taylor had not worked long or hard enough when in Rome, had allowed herself to be 'held up to scorn, ridicule and unfavourable publicity' as a result of the Burton affair, and moreover had continued afterwards 'to deride the quality of the film' in post-production interviews.

But not half as much as critics were soon to do:

The Burtons
with Sir
Michael
Redgrave at a
Royal
Command
Performance in
1965.

'overweight, overbosomed, overpaid and undertalented'
was one all too typical New York response to her performance, and although notices generally were more
enthusiastic about Harrison and Burton, it was perhaps
inevitable that a film which its director conceived in two
three-hour sections, and had then been hacked back to
four hours by other hands for its premiere, only to lose
another thirty minutes when the reviews came in, should
end up looking a little sketchy and confused. Perhaps the
most telling review came from Taylor herself who, after
hosting a screening of it in London shortly before the
official release, returned to the Dorchester Hotel and was
violently sick in the ladies' room.

But the Burtons, as they were soon to become, had
already moved on far from *Cleopatra*: in the year it had
taken to get the film from cutting-room to screen they had

both filed for divorce (Richard losing sight of his children for several months in the process) and begun to establish themselves as a couple of surviving sinners who, if they couldn't quite save the greatest asp disaster in the world, could at least turn around a modest little romance like *The VIPs* into a multi-million-dollar goldmine.

This meant that they once again had a reasonable selection of scripts at their hotel doors. Burton chose to go rapidly on to *Becket*, *Night of the Iguana* and a Broadway *Hamlet* directed by Gielgud, as if convinced that only a programme of staunchly classical or at any rate highbrow work in scripts by Anouilh, Tennessee Williams and Shakespeare could restore his image as a legitimate leading man. He still, in those early years of the alliance, burned with the passion to be taken seriously as an actor, whereas for Taylor the whole business had already become more than a little tedious. If *Cleopatra*, into which she had put so much of her time and energy over the last three years, was to end up a critical and commercial flop, then maybe she was at last better out of a business which had always been to her just that. Paradoxically, critics had missed the one central feature of that overblown movie: its title role, though played by an actress with far less dedication to the acting profession than either Vivien Leigh or Claudette Colbert who had been her most famous predecessors on the Nile, was actually rather better achieved because Liz managed to invade and overtake the part, to become Cleopatra in her full and wide-screen character rather than just giving a finer artist's impression.

But enough of that: better now, she thought, to follow Richard round the world while he carried an increasingly tatty and threadbare banner for thespians. What seems to have interested her far more than a career in these early Burton months was the intensity and complexity of their family situations and the need to sort all of them out, so that in the end even the aged Welsh relatives and acid London theatre people who took the view that Richard had sold out his honour and his reputation to a devilish combination of sex and money could eventually be won over, like her own children, to the prospect of yet another marriage. Not for the first time, the Taylor life seemed to be more intriguingly written and dynamically played than anything she was actually doing on screen.

But it all took time, and it wasn't until the pre-Broadway tour of *Hamlet* in 1964 that they were actually able to marry; by which time, some would argue, their best years were already almost over. Though most of his family and friends had now been won around to Liz, usually by her own insane generosity and single-minded determination that they were going to like her as the second Mrs Burton, Richard himself was still racked by a kind of matrimonial and professional guilt which kept him fairly close to the bottle and yet not close enough to the stage. Again and again he would repeat for journalists the story of Olivier telling him he would have to decide whether to be the greatest actor or the richest film star in the world, and of his reply that he had determined to be both; but every time he told it, somehow the likelihood of the double seemed to grow more and more distant.

Lord and Lady of the Rings.

The Burtons

'Even though there were rough
times, I wouldn't give up one
minute of my life with Richard
Burton: not a moment of the
ecstatic roller-coaster years of our
first marriage, nor of the ill-
starred attempt at a second go-
round'

That Broadway *Hamlet*, though directed by John Gielgud, seemed to me oddly insecure when compared to the one that Burton had given at the Old Vic less than a decade earlier. Yet, apart from *Faustus* with the Oxford students, it was to be his last stage appearance until *Equus* and the tragic attempts to make a come-back at the very end of his life with the catastrophic revivals of *Camelot* and *Private Lives*. Already, and as he stood just on the verge of his fortieth birthday, the second *Hamlet* was his edgy farewell to the greatness that had been so regularly forecast for him over the last fifteen years.

Not that Elizabeth saw any real problem or threat to their happiness there. Acting had always been something to do for a living, not anything to get really worked up about and least of all when real life was throwing everything else at you anyway. In the wake of *Cleopatra*, with *The VIPs* already on release, the most scandalous couple since the Windsors were able to attract queues outside hotels and stage doors wherever they went. Even his entire *Hamlet* seemed somehow only a curtain-raiser to the moment when she would come backstage afterwards to take him out for dinner, hotly pursued by all the photographers on Broadway and the somewhat bemused members of an otherwise fairly classical company unaccustomed to mounted police having to see them safely through the streets after the performance.

But for almost two years after *Cleopatra* and *The VIPs*, Taylor did virtually nothing but watch her husband work: through the English shooting of *Becket* (during which she filmed one short London television documentary reading poems taught her by Burton), through his Puerto Vallarta location for *Night of the Iguana* and then through Toronto and New York for *Hamlet*, she remained the faithful off-stage partner while still attracting vastly more press and public attention than anyone actually involved with Richard for any of the work he was doing in an increasingly determined attempt not to end up as the next Eddie Fisher.

It soon became clear, however, that the public wanted to see them together on screen as well as in all the tabloids. While it was arguable that Liz by her regular presence in the stalls sold more tickets to Burton's *Hamlet* than he did, there was a limit to how often that would work; while Burton alone, still unable to command anything like her now regular million-dollar-per-picture deals, could hardly be expected to carry the weight of all their present expenses and previous commitments. Something had therefore to be found for them to do together, to consolidate a remarkable change that had come over their public image. Whereas in Rome two years earlier people had spat at them in streets and the Vatican had denounced them, now in New York they emerged again as folk heroes. Had they not, after all, tried to live apart and failed? Had they then not sorted out the divorces, the children, the money and even managed to marry each other, thereby putting an almost fairy-tale ending on to an adulterous liaison? Had they not even survived the reviews for *Cleopatra*? New York liked all that: ever since Judy Garland at the Palace fifteen years earlier, Broadway had been where a huge Hollywood star could clamber back to public favour, and Taylor managed to do it without even having to appear on a stage except for one brief and bizarre charity performance at which she read some more poems taught her by Richard, who seemed to regard Dylan Thomas as the classical education Liz had never enjoyed.

She herself, always vastly more realistic than Richard, knew that several of those queuing for his *Hamlet* were not there for the Shakespeare, but she also knew that 'success is the greatest deodorant' and that they were on a high which could survive even *The Sandpiper*, a film of quite surprising awfulness given that the Burtons could at this moment in the mid-Sixties have had their pick of any script in Hollywood. This one concerned an artist living in a Big Sur beach house of considerable luxury with a tame bird ('I started out in *Lassie* working with animals twenty years ago, and here I am doing it again and I don't mean Richard,' said Taylor, who had now begun for the first time in her life to give some quite funny studio interviews), and then finding that a married Episcopalian minister has fallen in love with her. As with *The VIPs*, Metro seemed determined to nudge their audiences into thinking they were watching a glossily fictionalized account of life with the Burtons. In fact what they were watching here was a load of old B-picture romantic rubbish through which, said John Simon uncharitably, 'the ample Miss Taylor moves in a variety of ambulatory tents'. Other critics were not a lot kinder: Judith Crist worked out that, between them, the Burtons were getting a million and three-quarter dollars for the picture and thought that no one should have to agree to watch it for less, while Pauline Kael worried about Burton having to get his classical lips around such lines as 'I've lost all sense of sin' and 'I never knew what love was before.'

The curious thing about *The Sandpiper*, directed by Vincente Minnelli, who had put Elizabeth into *Father of the Bride* fifteen years earlier but was working now through a reverent haze of soft-focus celebrity, is the way in which Taylor actually thrives on its desperately inadequate script (by Dalton Trumbo, amazingly enough, and Michael Wilson), while Burton just manages to look shiftily embarrassed about it. Years of work in poor MGM vehicles often resembling hearses had left her even now with a kind of invulnerability to bad dialogue, while he could only make it seem still worse. Of the two, it is by no means true that he was invariably the better actor on

'Mr Burton and Miss Taylor were paid almost a million dollars each for performing in *The Sandpiper* (1965): if I were you, I wouldn't settle for less for watching them.' *New York Herald Tribune*

screen. He was only better when the material was good enough; when the chips were down, it was usually she who came through by turning the appalling into the merely awful.

Tynan may have dismissed *The Sandpiper* as the tale of a plump unmarried atheist and a stocky married clergyman going to bed on the coast of Upper California, but it took something like seven million dollars in America alone, breaking all the Radio City first-weekend records as crowds flocked to see the Burtons in the bedroom, one of the few sightings of them that had not been publicly available during their recent stay in New York. But at this point in the relationship, a number of contradictions were apparent: Burton was now doing on the side (in *Becket, Night of the Iguana, The Spy Who Came in from the Cold*) some of the best screen work he was ever to achieve, while Burton with Taylor (*The VIPs, The Sandpiper*) was unusually terrible. Yet the public only really wanted Burton as part of the Burtons. Taylor meanwhile, partly as a hangover from her Vatican denunciation and mainly because of her post-*Cleopatra* insistence on a million dollars a film, regardless of what that film was and how it was budgeted, was not getting the range of offers that he was, although the cinema remained primarily her natural habitat rather than his. Both knew there was a limit to how long they could live on a kind of airport celebrity, and both knew that given their huge family and other commitments (there were times when he seemed to be supporting most of Wales, while she looked after the residents of large areas of Israel, a legacy from her Todd/Fisher years) money was still often tight, which meant they were forever having to negotiate complex tax arrangements whereby, ludicrously, much of the Californian *Sandpiper* had to be shot in Paris.

Both set up Swiss residency and several multi-national tax shelters, and when even these proved insufficient Taylor decided to return at least notionally to the country of her birth and took up a British citizenship. Once again, she announced that she was simply doing this to form a closer union with the man she was married to at the time, and even she might perhaps have found it difficult to become entirely Welsh. But she had learnt enough to keep

this latest change of passport as quiet as possible, especially as it meant abjuring allegiance to the American flag under which most of her dollars were still earned. In truth, neither of them really had roots anywhere any more, which was why the neutrality and anonymity of Switzerland was as close as they ever came to a permanent home and shared financial base. If it was Hilton who first turned Liz into a wife, and Wilding who turned her into a mother, and Todd who turned her into a confident star, and Fisher who turned her into a Jewess, it was Burton who managed to turn her into a limited company. Not that he ever tried to hide his passion for money-making: when I once asked why they had gone into *The Sandpiper* and what it could possibly have been about, he looked at me in amazement and said it was about very nearly two million dollars, plus writing off some debts.

But what they had not yet enjoyed, and now most

'In *Who's Afraid of Virginia Woolf* [1966] . . . Elizabeth Taylor [gives] a remarkable performance: looking fat and fortyish, under a smear of make-up and with her voice pitched well below her belt, Liz as Martha is loud, sexy, vulgar, pungent and yet achieves moments of astonishing tenderness.' *Time*

needed, was some kind of a joint critical and commercial hit, and in one magical though never-repeatable year they managed to make, back to back, the only two real and total hits they ever achieved in a dozen tries over a decade. The first, Edward Albee's *Who's Afraid of Virginia Woolf?* was offered initially to Taylor alone; it had been around as a Broadway and London stage hit since 1962, and everyone from Ingrid Bergman through Bette Davis and Patricia Neal to Rosalind Russell had been cited as a possible Martha. When the producer Ernest Lehman announced that he was thinking of Taylor, the shock-horror was considerable and not only around California. Burton told his wife she was far too young for the role of the blowsy, sexy, vulgar, castrating campus shrew, and others told her more bluntly that she simply wasn't up to what has to be one of the greatest and most demanding roles written for a woman in the whole of American twentieth-century drama. But Elizabeth had always thrived on a challenge, and if she could pull this one off, she felt, she might at last win back some of the critical prestige she had begun to acquire at the time of *Cat* and *Suddenly Last Summer* almost a decade earlier; after all there was no reason to go on forever playing the dumb film star to her husband's classical actor, and this would surely be the chance to prove that, contrary to widespread

European belief, he had not in fact married beneath him.

With Taylor hooked on Martha, it didn't take long for Lehman to come around to Burton for the wimpish, academic husband. The role had already been rejected outright by Henry Fonda, and though Cary Grant and James Mason were briefly considered, Burton eventually won through on the old theory that as a couple the Burtons remained unbeatable box-office. With Mike Nichols making his début as a film director, and George Segal and Sandy Dennis cast as the unfortunate other couple for Albee's psychological game of get-the-guests, work started in July 1965 on a rehearsal stage where the company spent three weeks before a single camera was moved into place.

Shooting then on a totally closed set with a deeply theatrical intensity, Nichols came up with the most expensive black-and-white movie ever made (at five million dollars) but also the one on which most claims for the Burtons as a serious acting couple now rest. If not as strong or secure as Uta Hagen and Arthur Hill in the New York original, they did manage to turn in warts-and-all performances of truly monstrous authority, brawling their way through Albee's orgy of torn egos and phantom children and marital degradation with a technical authority and ravaged strength that amazed their doubters. Both were heavily tipped for Oscars, though in the event Burton and the film lost out to Paul Scofield and *A Man for All Seasons*, leaving Taylor somewhat indignantly alone with her second and, thus far, last Academy Award.

Respectably established at last as the nearest that Hollywood would ever get to the Broadway Lunts or the Stratford Oliviers of the 1950s, the Burtons now proceeded to make the other great film of their partnership and in its way the flip side of *Virginia Woolf*. En route to Rome for *Taming of the Shrew*, they did however find time to stop off first in New York, where Elizabeth published a brief autobiography of truly numbing dullness, and then in Oxford where Burton had promised his old tutor, Nevill Coghill, that he would do something to raise much-needed money for the local Playhouse and the Oxford University Dramatic Society. Having recently been its secretary, I was remotely involved in one or two early discussions with Coghill as to what Burton might actually be willing to do on stage, and we were (as I recall) more than ready to settle for a Sunday-night reading of the usual Dylan Thomas when he announced from America that he would be willing to play *Doctor Faustus* with an undergraduate cast and Nevill directing, provided that he didn't have to do it for more than a week. Oh yes, he added, and Elizabeth would be willing to appear as a mute Helen of Troy.

By the time they got around to doing it I had left the university and gone abroad, but the idea remained riveting: here was an ex-Oxford undergraduate, now married to the most famous woman in the world, still under attack for having sold out his artistic soul to her celebrity and fortune, willing to take on the one classic drama which actually deals with those themes and moreover to have her in it with him and then put the proceeds to the benefit of the old academic life that he often pretended to regret and threatened to return to in old age as a visiting professor.

The only trouble was that they actually did it very badly. Insufficient rehearsal time, chaotic student performances and a general Oxford failure to align an OUDS way of life with that of unusually starry guests led to some very mixed reviews of which the general tenor was that the only deadly sin inflicted by Mephistopheles thoughout the evening was that of terminal boredom. Still, a debt to his Oxford education had been paid off, and if only Burton hadn't decided to film it a few months later the whole shambles could have been written off to generosity and experience.

On then to Rome, where the paparazzi were gathered to await their first real treat since *Cleopatra* had wrapped there four summers earlier; this time, though, things were a little different. The Burtons who had left the holy city as scandalous adulterers were returning as the most regally married couple in the business; having left with an epic fiasco like *Cleopatra*, they were also returning to the vastly more classical respectability of William Shakespeare's *Taming of the Shrew* as directed by one of the most renowned Italian stage artists Franco Zeffirelli, here making his movie début with a project he'd initially conceived for Marcello Mastroianni and Sophia Loren.

But after slugging it out through *Virginia Woolf*, the Burtons were in good training for Petruchio and Katharina. Much helped by a literate and witty screen treatment from Paul Dehn and others, not to mention Zeffirelli's operatic and scenic talent for feasting the eye and the ear on spectacle and sound, they turned in a sumptuous *Shrew* which often looked like *Kiss Me Kate* without the songs but was none the worse for all that. This is not, after all, a sombre classic like *Faustus* or even *Virginia Woolf*: it's a joyous romp, and for the first and last time on screen the Burtons managed to convey a kind of infectious delight in brawling their way into bed.

One or two purist reviews talked of a betrayal of Shakespeare, or of the Burtons' apparent inability to overcome all the subsidiary activity with which Zeffirelli surrounded them, or of a supporting cast (Cyril Cusack, Michael Hordern, Alan Webb) vastly more authoritative than they were; but by and large this was recognized as a rich and rare treat, and maybe even the liveliest handling of Shakespeare on screen since Olivier's *Henry V* all of twenty years earlier. Sadly it was to mark not only the high point but also the end of the Burtons as an interesting or bankable screen team.

'Having had at one another very roundly and seriously in *Virginia Woolf*, the Burtons are now in *The Taming of the Shrew* [1967] turned loose with slapsticks for a forthrightly campy entertainment refereed by Franco Zeffirelli out of the corner of one winking eye.' *New York Times*

They were to stay married, or briefly remarried, for nearly another decade; but after their triumphant return to Rome, where it had all started, the next ten years were to be an increasing agony of decline and often alcoholic despair as first of all their public and then they themselves began to lose faith in their continued possibilities as a couple on screen or off. Together they were to make another five films and a brief television series, all of which lost money; apart, Burton briefly managed to scramble back with *Where Eagles Dare* and *Anne of the Thousand Days*, but Taylor did not find another box-office winner after the *Shrew* until an Agatha Christie thriller (*The Mirror Crack'd*) all of fifteen years later.

Ironically enough, at this very moment, when with the *Shrew* and *Virginia Woolf* they had taught themselves how to work together superbly on camera, the public suddenly began to lose interest in the idea of the Burtons altogether. Their fame had always rested on a form of gossip-column sensationalism: now they seemed about to turn into Hollywood's golden couple, advancing towards a safe old age in more and more respectable work, and that was somehow not what was wanted or expected of them at all. If there were to be no more midnight calls to the hospital, or irate ex-partners, or complex divorce and adoption settlements, then the public decided that it would drift off in search of excitement elsewhere.

In this they were admittedly encouraged by Burton's dogged determination to film his Oxford *Faustus*, a project that had now become so obsessive that he even invested a million of his own dollars when American distributors declined to take the risk. Co-directing with Coghill, again using Oxford undergraduates (among them a young Maria Aitken) and his wife for the supporting cast, he shot the film in Rome and London and then spent a year trying to find an American production company willing to release it. From the glory of the *Shrew* he had gone into what *Variety* called 'one of the most desperately non-commercial enterprises in the history of motion pictures', and somehow neither of the Burtons ever quite seemed to recover from the shock of discovering that they alone were no longer enough to save a picture. Considering that they had personally retrieved *The Sand-*

piper at the box-office, it came as a rude awakening to find they couldn't repeat the miracle for what was still, even after they had finished with it, a rather better text. In the end, *Faustus* was Richard's undoing but not in quite the way that the original plot dictated.

But given that there was always a time-lag of about a year between the shooting of a picture and its box-office accounting, it took a while for this abrupt change in the Burtons' public image and profitability to dawn on them and their employers. For now, while he unusually waited on the sidelines, Liz went straight on from *Faustus* to *Reflections in a Golden Eye*, the Carson McCullers tale of murder and repressed homosexuality on an army station in Georgia. This was a project that she'd taken on for that most frequent and favourite of her contract reasons, because it offered a marvellous role to her great movie ally Montgomery Clift, who was once again in all kinds of drink and drugs trouble. This time, however, he died of that trouble before shooting could start, leaving Taylor to mourn the closest of all her professional friendships and to announce that she would only consider going ahead if Marlon Brando could be signed as Clift's replacement. Considering Brando's usual reluctance to work, this was widely reckoned to be a manoeuvre whereby Liz could avoid doing the film altogether in the absence of Clift; but Brando immediately accepted the offer, even agreeing that Taylor could take top billing and rather more loot (her usual million dollars to his three-quarters), and John Huston was left to bring together two undoubtedly charismatic stars in a script that seemed to suit neither of them very well.

Huston had encountered Taylor when she was still married to Fisher but accompanying Burton on to the *Night of the Iguana* location, while arranging for Michael Wilding to be her agent; John found the array of past, present and future husbands somewhat confusing, and on one occasion had solemnly presented Elizabeth with a gun and several bullets inscribed with the names of the rest of the *Iguana* cast in case the whole thing got to be too much for her.

Professionally they now got along very well, Huston reckoning her one of the finest actresses even he had ever

With Marlon Brando; and with Brian Keith and director John Huston on the set of *Reflections in a Golden Eye* (1967): 'a stupefying mishmash of Southern clichés.' *Saturday Review*

worked with; but the story that Carson McCullers herself had once called 'a pretentious piece of gothic' was photographed in much the same tradition, with Brando proving largely incomprehensible through a mouthful of deep-Southern vowels and Taylor offering a spirited re-run of her previous Tennessee Williams performances, only this time in a plot which required her in all solemnity to announce that her lover's wife had just cut off her own nipples with a pair of gardening shears.

If the reviews here were no worse than for *Dr Faustus*, where Burton had confused several of his critics by adding bits of *Tamburlaine* and old Shakespearian film clips to liven up a tricky text, they were certainly not a lot better, and by the time these two movies were released (or in the case of *Faustus* secreted) it was evident that the Burtons were suddenly in a lot of trouble at the box-office, the one place where until now they had managed to get out of all their other marital and fiscal problems. Ironically, some of Taylor's best performances were being given at precisely the moment when the public had suddenly started to lose interest in her on the screen. The accumulation of gossip-column sagas over the past decade was at last leading to a kind of Burton overkill, whereby people had seen and heard so much of them that there was really no longer any urge to pay good money and see their films as well. Why go out and queue for those, when the stars were all too available at airports and in hotel lobbies via fan magazines and an almost daily series of no less dramatic newspaper and television news-bulletin pictures? They had become part of the permanent paparazzi landscape, and the price they paid for such a Faustian bargain was that they could no longer be taken very seriously by critics or audiences, even when they were working well.

None of that might have much mattered if either Elizabeth or Richard at this time had been able to develop a clear idea of what they really wanted to do with their careers. For her, movie-making was still often a boring means of paying the rent: having never had to fight for stardom, she had no real knowledge of how to hang on to it as she now began rapidly to disappear from the top ten box-office listings. For him, movie stardom was still somehow unreal and unimportant compared to what he

had left behind him on stage. Both of them were by now locked into the cinema, but neither of them seemed to have the passion or the long-haul conditioning to fight for their places there, and as a result they began slowly but surely to lose touch with an industry of which they had become the last married megastars.

At first the fall from grace was concealed, at least partially, by the calibre of the people they were still able to work with. The Burtons at this time attracted classy projects (both Isherwood and Coppola had worked at various drafts of the *Reflections* screenplay); and after the Huston picture she rejoined Burton for *The Comedians*, which also had an impressive pedigree: screenplay by Graham Greene from his own novel about the Englishmen caught up in Haiti under Papa Doc Duvalier's regime, cast to include not only the Burtons but Alec Guinness, Peter Ustinov and Lillian Gish.

Here again, though, a well-known book began to fall apart in front of the cameras: the story that the Haitian ambassador to the USA was to call 'an inflammatory libel publicly released to mislead the American people' did indeed manage to suggest that the Duvalier regime was perhaps less than totally liberal-democratic in its random use of a killer force of Tontons Macoute, but something went terribly wrong with the central casting of Richard as a reluctantly rebellious hotelier and Elizabeth as the ambassador's wife he comes to love. For the London *Times*, David Robinson reckoned that 'the Burtons are

On *The Comedians* set (1967), with Burton, director Peter Glenville and Alec Guinness; and with Peter Ustinov: 'an only moderately interesting account of apathy and personal self-indulgence in the midst of a nation undergoing terrible trial.' *New York Times*

153

quite the most extraordinary phenomenon in pictures today. A stocky couple, courting premature middle age, they are nobody's ideal of young romance, despite Elizabeth Taylor's extraordinarily beautiful features, and their acting hardly seems to matter . . . the whole reason for their attraction remains obscure: but a partial, likely explanation is the publicized turbulence of their off-screen lives, the disdain for convention and disregard for opinion that, even in an age of discarded conventions, has a grandeur and glamour and uniqueness.'

Not enough, though, to matter at the box-office where, like *Reflections* and *Faustus*, *The Comedians* went down very badly indeed. Intriguingly it was Peter Ustinov, playing Taylor's husband in the film, who first pinpointed the real impossibility of their position even at the precise moment when Liz (though forbidden by Burton to attend the ceremony) was being honoured with her second best

'No sooner does the plot of *The Comedians* begin to move than we are brought to a dead halt by the Burtons' cinematic amours and maulings.'
Chicago Sun

actress Oscar for her part in *Who's Afraid of Virginia Woolf*:

'In my opinion the chemistry of having them both in a film, though regarded as a rare coup by financiers, in fact lacked mystery. Love scenes and, even worse, lust scenes between people who presumably have them anyway in the privacy of their own homes are inevitably somewhat flat on the screen, and if they happen to be passing through a momentary crisis such scenes are worse than flat, merely a tribute to their professionalism, and there are few things worse than that. Richard is a fine actor with a wayward quality women find hard to resist, but the waywardness is somehow stunted by the image of off-screen propriety in opulent wealth. Elizabeth, too, a person of tremendous instinct and surprising intelligence, requires a latitude which the outward appurtenances of the superstar somehow blunt.'

In truth, as Ustinov was perhaps too charitable to point out, the Burtons had in less than a decade royally progressed from being the Hollywood Windsors to being some kind of middle-European Queen Mother and her consort, and the switchover from doomed romantics to affluent registered private companies did them a lot of damage among the younger audiences who were already making up most of the cinema crowds around the world. A review in *Variety* that led off 'plodding, low-key, tedious, routine and seemingly interminable' could have been referring to any of the twelve films that Taylor made between *Faustus* in 1967 and *A Little Night Music* eleven long and artistically catastrophic years later: in fact it was their notice of *The Comedians*.

Undeterred (especially since the reviews had not yet appeared), the Burtons decided to crank the double-act into life one more time before starting on a long professional and eventually private separation. For this next film there would be a return to Tennessee Williams, though not for anything so distinguished as *Cat* or *Suddenly Last Summer*; instead, *Boom!* was cobbled together from one of his short stories (*Man Bring Up This Road*) and a play that had already flopped on Broadway (*The Milk Train Doesn't Stop Here Any More*). By now the director Joseph Losey had acquired the property, retitled *Boom!* as a reflection not of the way it would explode into disaster but rather of the sound made by the waves crashing into Flora Goforth's seaside castle, and was hoping to make it with Simone Signoret and Sean Connery.

When that plan fell through, Losey was reluctantly persuaded that it might do for the Burtons, though early dealings with them warned him of the dangers of 'sacred cows and super monsters' who failed to turn up on time or even in the right country for production meetings. A necrophiliac tale of a much-married millionairess ('There is nothing funny about the story of my life,' said Liz when Losey was trying to persuade her to play it for comedy) and the doomed poet who comes to nudge her on to death, this was always a baroque and gothically terrible little script mainly recalled for the way in which Hermione Baddeley had played it on stage as an over-the-top parody of Tallulah Bankhead.

That route was clearly not open to Taylor, who instead plays Flora Goforth for real, thereby reducing an eccentric folly to a leaden debate between herself and Burton as the angel of death, though the lugubrious fable was fleetingly enlivened by Noël Coward as the neighbouring Witch of Capri, a role created on stage by Mildred Dunnock. For Noël, as he wrote in the Coward Diaries, '. . . it was an enjoyable experience: I love Liz Taylor and found her a million per cent professional and wonderful to work with. Richard, of course, was sweet and the director Joe Losey a dear man. I had a bit of trouble with Tennessee's curiously phrased dialogue, but apart from that everything was halcyon.'

A few months later, having seen a rough-cut, he was not so certain: 'I'm not sure whether or not it will storm the world, but I'm quite good and look all right.' The rest of the film sadly didn't: Losey himself thought it was necrophiliac and believed he was the first person ever to make a picture with the Burtons that lost money, though in fact he only came third to the directors of *Doctor Faustus* and *The Comedians*. But he got off to a tricky start on the Sardinia location ('the Burtons arrived both screaming drunk and abusive and it was unimaginably awful'), and had to do thirteen takes on their first scene. Later they got along rather better, though Losey never

quite came around to Taylor: 'She has exquisite eyes, exquisite skin and in many ways she was then a most beautiful woman. But she's got a bad figure, she doesn't take care of it, she has chubby hands, is short and she's got a common accent. I knew that the first problem would be clothes, because she always wears clothes that accentuate the fact that she's short and fat instead of the opposite.'

The second and still greater problem with *Boom!* was, as Losey said, that 'there is this curious dichotomy between the Burtons and me: they are highly-paid, commercial, big stars and I am not ... so even though we eventually succeeded in working well together, one is still confronted by a preconditioned public that expects something from them and something from me and the two do not mix.'

Williams himself politely reckoned that the film was 'garbage', and his view was echoed by critics around the world, who had now really started to take the Burtons apart: 'When people reach a certain status in showbiz,' thought the critic of *Life*, 'a kind of arrogance seems to set in. They get to thinking, perhaps unconsciously, that they can dare us to reject anything they feel like shovelling out . . . there is a tired, slack quality in most of the Burtons' work that is by now a form of insult. They don't so much act as deign to appear before us, and there is neither discipline nor dignity in what they do. She is fat and will do nothing with her most glaring defect, an unpleasant voice which she cannot adequately control. He conversely acts with nothing but his voice, rolling out his lines with much elegance but no feeling at all.'

By now, even Richard and Elizabeth could take the hint that it was time to go their separate ways on screen, if not yet in life itself; over the next five years they only ever made two more films together, and both of those were equally catastrophic at the box-office: the gold of their *Cleopatra* affair had at last tarnished beyond any kind of restoration.

For a while it looked as though Burton might be able to go it alone (*Where Eagles Dare* and *Anne of the Thousand Days* were both late-Sixties commercial winners for him); but for Taylor there was to be nothing but a relentless succession of a dozen more losers stretching right the way through the 1970s. For a while this seems not to have strained the marriage unduly, especially as Elizabeth's interest in films and filming had never really regained the high ground of *Virginia Woolf*. For someone of what she was always the first to describe as limited acting talent, she knew enough about the business and its screenplays to recognize that she had already probably done the best work she was ever going to do on camera. The intensity was still apparent (as Coward said, 'She is always there, you never ever look up to find her staring fixedly at your forehead') but the ambition to prove herself had been achieved, and somehow there wasn't a lot now left to do.

The curiosity of the Burton crash was how fast it came: just as the reviews for *Boom!* in 1968 were putting an end to any further thoughts of an artistic partnership, Hollywood released its figures for the previous year (the year of *Virginia Woolf* and the *Shrew* on general release) showing that fifty per cent of all American box-office income in 1966–67 had been made from movies starring one or other or both of the Burtons.

Those days, however, were now at an end, and the five years leading up to the first Burton divorce were for them both a kind of slow landslide into appalling movies, personal tragedies (she lost her father, he suffered the near-paralysis of a beloved brother), frequent returns to hospital and then desperate attempts to stay in the headlines with spectacularly bad-taste parties and ever larger diamonds. Something had obviously gone terribly wrong, and among the onlookers, both friendly and critical, there was a headlong rush back to the old adage about not praying for fame and fortune too loudly in case your prayer is granted. Watching Richard and Elizabeth in these years was rather like watching a couple of drunken drivers lurching around the world from one accident to another.

Along the way, both managed to keep working in a semi-detached sort of fashion: Liz went straight from *Boom!* into another Joe Losey calamity, *Secret Ceremony*, for which once again she was not his first choice. Meant originally for Ingrid Bergman, this was a bizarre little horror about a middle-aged London prostitute and the orphan girl (Mia Farrow, wide-eyed and hot from *Rosemary's Baby*) who picks her up because she resembles her dead mother; Robert Mitchum was also in there somewhere as a child-molesting stepfather, and there were strong suggestions that Taylor and Farrow were having a lesbian affair, though most of that got heavily deleted when the film was eventually sold to television. It also made history in being the first film ever to have long new scenes (though not made by the original cast or director) added in order to make it both acceptable and widely comprehensible on the small screen but by then nothing could undo the damage of the reviews, which for Taylor hit the jugular in their savagery: 'Her disintegration,' wrote Rex Reed for *Holiday*, 'is a very sad thing to stand by helplessly and watch, but something ghastly has happened over the course of her last four or five films ... Taylor has become a hideous parody of herself – a fat, sloppy, yelling, screeching banshee.'

With reviews like that, and nothing but derision from Burton and his producer Hal Wallis when she suggested that she might play the young Anne Boleyn to Richard's

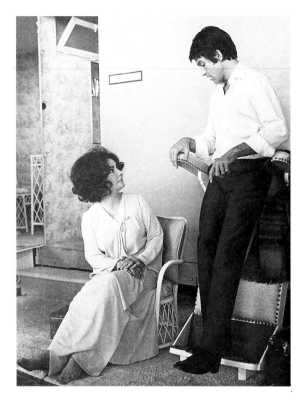

With Warren Beatty for *The Only Game in Town* (1970); and with Mia Farrow in *Secret Ceremony* (1968).

Henry VIII in the forthcoming *Anne of the Thousand Days*, Elizabeth took the hint that her movie-making days were perhaps now drawing to a close. On the other hand, she was still, if amazingly, two years away from a fortieth birthday, and there wasn't a lot else she could do. The children were not only growing up but marrying fast, her elder son by Wilding was about to make her a grandmother, and there was a limit to the amount of time she could spend hovering around a film set wondering if Richard was about to revert to type and go to bed with his next leading lady. Alternatively she could go shopping or move hotels, but not a lot else ever interested her very much. For all its irritations she had been a child of the studio system, and now the system had let her down badly by simply not being there any more. The star factory had closed, leaving its last great creation wondering what she was supposed to do next.

Television, maybe; despite the butchering of *Secret Ceremony*, there was surely an audience out there somewhere who would like a look at Taylor by their own firesides. Accordingly she did a guest shot (with Burton) on a Sammy Davis show and then made a tribute to Mike Todd, whose *Around the World*, in which she still had a considerable percentage, was about to go out on the small screen for the first time. It soon became clear, though, that no new career was going to be possible for her on video; like so many of the great old studio stars, she was too big for television and oddly uneasy with a medium which, instead of projecting her several times larger than life, could actually reduce her to kneecap height. As at some deeply uneasy press conferences over the years, the whole immediacy of the new medium terrified her: television, like the paparazzi, came in too fast and too close and nobody ever seemed to do retakes or touch up the prints. Taylor on television is much like Sir Herbert Beerbohm Tree on a gramophone record: the new medium is just wrong for the old training, and it wasn't until the mid-1980s, when she began working in television films rather than on videotape, that she found a way to conquer the technology once again.

And yet, to misquote *Cleopatra*, she was Elizabeth Taylor still. Film-makers faced with her plummeting box-office records understandably took the view that maybe that had been the fault of the movies she had chosen, that maybe if they could find her another half-way adequate script and an impressive co-star this trend could yet be reversed, and she could somewhere earn the million dollars she was still demanding. Thus it was that George Stevens, the veteran director who had given her two great hits in *Giant* and *A Place in the Sun*, put her up for *The Only Game in Town* opposite the singer she had once been rumoured to have had an affair with in the declining months of the Wilding marriage, Frank Sinatra. Though it had flopped badly as a play on Broadway, this was an intriguing Frank Gilroy script about a couple of Las Vegas losers finding each other and marriage, the 'only game' of the title, and with Sinatra it might just have worked out well enough. But this was to be another bad year for Taylor, who spent much of it in a London hospital for a hysterectomy while Burton was being sacked for 'consistent lateness' from a Tony Richardson movie called *Laughter in the Dark*, which admittedly he was well out of. By the time they got to Paris in the autumn, *The Only*

Game in Town had been forcibly delayed by three months and Sinatra had pulled out altogether, leaving Warren Beatty to come in from an altogether different generation and acting tradition. Both he and Elizabeth did in fact achieve, despite Stevens's desperately ponderous direction, a light-comedy technique which was engaging and often unexpected; but reviews were again bad-to-worse, and nothing could now save a downward spiral on Taylor films whereby this one barely made back worldwide the million and a half dollars they had given her to make it. For two years thereafter, she went into total screen retirement, drifting around the world with Burton while he worked, persistently announcing to the press after several highly-publicized fights that there was nothing wrong with their marriage give or take a little volatility among highly-strung artists, and then more privately trying to deal with an increasingly agonizing back condition.

But the Burtons had by now become a curious parody of themselves: indeed by 1970 they were to be found doing farcical guest-shots on a *Lucille Ball Show* for no apparent reason, and by the time of her fortieth birthday in 1972 Liz was most famous as the bearer of a one-million-dollar diamond ring which had actually been exhibited in the window of Cartiers and was, in the view of the *New York Times*, proof that 'in an age of war and poverty it gets harder every day to scale the heights of true vulgarity, though given some loose millions it can be done and, worse, admired.'

The actual party for her fortieth, in February 1972, was given by Liz at a hotel in Budapest where Burton was at the time filming a remarkably terrible *Bluebeard*, and at a cost which could probably have kept most of Hungary in food and drink for several weeks thereafter. Indeed such was the outcry even in the capitalist press that the Burtons were then forced to donate an equal amount to charity. Thus it was that a delighted Peter Ustinov on behalf of UNICEF received a cheque for $45,000.

But because neither Richard nor Elizabeth now seemed capable of making films that were anything other than risible in their inadequacy, they had become fair targets for every Anglo-American gossip columnist, agony aunt

With Peter
O'Toole in
*Under Milk
Wood* (1971);
and as Jimmie
Jean Jackson in
*Hammersmith is
Out* (1972).

and even leader writer with a thin day and a deadline and
nothing much else to complain about except gross extravagance as exhibited by the last two people on earth who
could apparently afford to indulge themselves in it.

When the last of the big spenders did get back to the
screen again, it was for another sextet of artistic and
commercial disasters culminating in an all-too-prophetic
television film entitled *Divorce His, Divorce Hers.* Before
that, in a final burst of literary endeavour, she and
Richard joined Peter O'Toole and Glynis Johns for
Andrew Sinclair's film version of *Under Milk Wood,* in
which Taylor played a somewhat improbable Rosie Pro-
bert, 'cosmeticized and fineried', thought Stanley Kauff-
man, 'to look less like a small-town Welsh whore than
part of a deal which also included Burton.'

From that loser she went straight to *Zee and Co,* known
in America as *X, Y and Zee* and based on the story by
Edna O'Brien (in fact an original screenplay) about an
unfaithful architect and the wife who finally takes his
mistress to his own bed. Michael Caine as the architect
and Susannah York as the mistress surrounded Taylor
with a couple of strong performances, while Liz herself
warmed over her Martha from *Virginia Woolf* to arrive at
another loud-mouthed monster; but for the *New Yorker*
Pauline Kael was appalled: 'She has changed before our
eyes from the fragile child with a woman's face to this
great bawd. Maybe child actresses don't quite grow up if
they stay in the movies; maybe that's why from ingénue-

With Richard Burton in the all too accurately titled *Divorce His, Divorce Hers* (1973).

goddess she went right over the hill. The change in her is not unlike the change in Judy Garland.'

Unlike Garland, however, or at the upper end of the cultural scale the Vivien Leigh whom Taylor often also resembled – and not only because they had both been through the *Cleopatra* nightmare on screen – Elizabeth was a fighter and a survivor. The work and the marriage might well be falling apart, but she herself had a kind of relentless determination to slug it out with whatever husbands or screenplays or critics the fates might throw at her. MGM children didn't often quit: like the army, the long studio contracts of the 1950s created marathon runners who, while they occasionally had to clamber over the bodies of dropouts like Monroe and Garland, could usually then manage to last the course. In that sense Taylor, like Ronald Reagan, could go on for ever: Mother Courage doesn't leave the stage half-way through Act Two, even if it is proving to be an unusually tricky audience.

It was Molly Haskell, writing in the *Village Voice* of *Hammersmith is Out*, the next and mercifully penultimate Burton fiasco-film (a black comedy directed by Peter Ustinov abut an escaped mental patient and a deep-Southern waitress, for neither of which roles they seemed plausible casting), who pinpointed the change in Taylor and the essential reason why she was not going to fall apart as fast as her current movies: 'She was a product of the fake-fabulous Fifties, when movie stars really were products and when the idea of sensuality preceded its essence. Some actresses killed themselves over that discrepancy. Taylor was made of harder stuff. She began with a period of maximum beauty and minimum talent, survived a time when she was just a dazzling embarrassment, and has made it with colors and cusswords flying to the present. At last her essence seems to have caught up with her image, and she has relaxed into one ripe, raucous, caterwauling paper tigress of a woman.'

All of which was true, but didn't solve the problem that movie audiences were unprepared and unwilling to pay for ripe and raucous paper tigers, especially at a time when the movies themselves appeared to be on almost the last of their legs. Financiers were nearly as hard to find as paying customers: the millionaire manufacturer of large numbers of American caravans had in fact paid for (and lost) the entire budget of *Hammersmith*, while for Taylor's next disaster, a little thriller called *Night Watch*, they had to get the money from a perfume company which also then lost it very rapidly indeed.

By now Richard's career had also collapsed into such horrors as *Bluebeard* and *The Assassination of Trotsky*; he was heavily back to the bottle, mourning the death of a brother and the loss of any real professional credibility or bankability, reverting to his old infidelities and generally allowing a marriage that Elizabeth still cared about and believed in to disintegrate into a series of prolonged public squabbles. But having always lived that marriage in the full glare of the cameras, there was a certain ghastly logic in ending it there. The last film which was to star the Burtons together, one originally made as a two-part television drama for Harlech, the Welsh ITV company in which they owned several thousand shares, was called *Divorce His, Divorce Hers*, and by the time it reached a few reluctant cinemas and television stations in the latter part of 1973, the two stars had already announced a formal separation.

Mother Courage in Sables

'For those who grew up in love with Elizabeth Taylor . . . it is good to report that after years of bad directors and rotten scripts she is once again the kind of star that marquees light up for: gone is the screeching voice and the truckdriver's slump' *New York Daily News*

Though it may have seemed to newspaper readers around the world like a lot longer, the Burtons had been together for barely a decade at the time Elizabeth announced their first separation in July 1973; it then took them another three years, including a second marriage to each other, before that separation became final, though they were still working together on stage a year or so before Burton's sudden death in 1984. In the meantime, like a couple of punch-drunk prizefighters, they continued through marriages to other people to lurch around the world, apparently unable to live together but equally unable to live apart until in the closing months of his life Richard alone found a marriage that might have worked. It was always an uneasy spectacle, made worse by a gleeful press and the fact that the whole concept of the Burtons now seemed to belong to a lost era of 1960s tolerance and unaccountable extravagance. By the mid-1970s the accountants had taken over, and both Richard and Elizabeth were somehow looking as beached and bloated as hot-air balloons after the invention of the aeroplane.

The fact that neither of them could get their careers off the ground sent Richard back to the bottle and a series of increasingly indiscreet off-camera liaisons, while Elizabeth seemed now to recognize that yet another new beginning was called for: she slimmed down, went for relatively little money into a romantic soap-opera about the wonders of plastic surgery called *Ash Wednesday*, and then formally announced that she and her husband were better off apart, adding 'pray for us' — presumably in recognition that their partnership had become a kind of religion to film fans around the globe.

The rest of that year was largely taken up with airport reconciliations, further separation announcements, rumours of fresh liaisons (Aristotle Onassis was now widely tipped as Taylor's sixth husband), and then another bedside rethink of the scenario when, in December, Liz was admitted to the UCLA hospital in Los Angeles for major surgery on her ovaries. They survived another Christmas together, but by the June of 1974 Taylor was in a Gstaad courtroom telling the judge that she had tried everything and failed in her attempts to keep

167

The Burtons in 1971, arriving in England to see her first grandchild; and Taylor with Henry Fonda in *Ash Wednesday* (1973).

the marriage alive. Over its closing months she had filmed some narrative links for a glossy compilation of old clips (*That's Entertainment*) glued together to celebrate the MGM studios which for eighteen years had been her home, and then gone to Munich for her first totally European venture, a macabre little shocker about a woman going mad. Variously known as *The Driver's Seat* (the title of the Muriel Spark novella on which it was based) or *Identikit*, this marked an all-time low in the Taylor career, one for which its distributors were able to find virtually no cinema or television outlets of any kind.

Privately, on the other hand, the divorce from Burton seemed to release a new energy in her, as she swung straight into an affair with Henry Wynberg, a forty-year-old used car salesman who looked for a long time the most likely candidate for her sixth wedding. Still paying regular hospital visits to deal with an always bad back and ceaseless internal complications, aware that even when she was well there wasn't a lot of point in making movies which never even got released, she returned for a while to the New York nightclub circuit, where Truman Capote found her lamenting the end of the best of her marriages: 'You don't always fry the fish you want to fry: some of the men I would most have wanted to marry just weren't interested in women. But Richard was the one most worth quarrelling with. Emlyn Williams once told him he'd been a fool to marry me when he could have been a great actor and I was just a movie star nothing, but the important thing is what happens when two people love each other. He thought I drank too much and I knew he did, but I was usually just trying to keep up, to get to wherever he was . . . the trouble is that when you find what you've always wanted, that's the beginning of the end.'

But it was still to be a slow process: within a year of the divorce they were back together again, though not before Liz had evicted Wynberg (who went on to face some unattractive criminal prosecutions relating to his earlier life) and spent a chilly winter in Leningrad with George Cukor making the most expensive musical ever, a twelve-million-dollar Soviet-American fiasco called *The Blue Bird*, through which she suffered amoebic dysentery, chronic back troubles and one of the worst screenplays of modern times. Her appearance in a quartet of roles ('Mother', 'Maternal Love', 'Light' and 'The Blue Fairy') was perhaps best summarized by Penelope Gilliatt: 'First seen wearing a granny shawl and a mobcap, she next turns up as the Witch in a Jimmy Durante nose and then more recognizably as Light, on whom diamonds seem to have gone berserk, hanging like ringlets from every inch of hair and ear.'

'Not so much a movie as a covenant with boredom' (*New York Times*), *The Blue Bird* was a co-production nightmare in which Cukor found himself working with an all-star cast (Taylor, Ava Gardner, Jane Fonda, Cicely Tyson, Robert Morley) but a largely Soviet crew who inspired something less than confidence. When Cukor told them how proud he was to be filming in the very same studio where Eisenstein had made *Battleship Potemkin* in 1925 the interpreter beamed with pleasure: 'Yes Mr Cukor,' he replied, 'and with much of the very same equipment we are using now.'

A prolonged Russian incarceration did however give Taylor the time to reconsider her Burton years, and by the time she was released from Leningrad she had decided that they were 'joined together at the hip' and should remarry as soon as possible. Burton to his credit had considerable doubts about this plan; he had managed to dry out over the past few months, and took the view that maybe the most they should now try for would be occasional periods of living together, released from the permanent bonds of a marriage that had evidently driven them both to the brink of destruction. But Taylor still only ever recognized a marriage, and by October 1975 she had convinced him that they were either destined or doomed to stay together for ever, 'stuck like chicken feathers to tar' as she put it in a widely-released love letter to him. After a bizarre journey to the Wailing Wall in Israel (since both were now claiming Jewish ancestry) and a charity tennis tournament in Johannesburg, they finally remarried by a river in Botswana where they hoped to be alone, give or take a couple of hundred photographers.

'Sturm has remarried Drang,' noted the *Boston Globe*, 'and all is right with the world' – except of course that it wasn't. The strain of a remarriage and his fiftieth birthday which fell soon afterwards had driven Richard straight back to the bottle, and after a few uneasy weeks back at the Swiss chalet he fell deeply in love with a neighbour there, Susan Hunt, who was to be his next wife and provide, among several drying-out cures, an escape route from the all-embracing Elizabeth. She, meanwhile, alternately chastened and enraged by the failure of yet another marriage and the need therefore to apply for a fifth divorce (though only her second from Burton), went briefly back to Henry Wynberg and then reconsidered her position. Clearly the new escort would not do for a long-term alliance, and equally clearly nobody in movies or even television was begging her to return to an acting career. Something would have to be done, but she was not entirely sure quite what, and in the meantime her temper was not much improved by the fact that Burton had been straightened out and sobered up so fast by Mrs Hunt that within a few weeks he was back on the Broadway stage for the first time in a decade, with an extremely impressive performance as the psychiatrist in Shaffer's *Equus*, one he later filmed.

An irritable Taylor went from Wynberg into another brief affair, this one with an Iranian diplomat, then

Back in London after her sixth marriage and her second to Burton (1975).

seemed suddenly to acquire a taste for the political life. At a Bicentennial dinner in July 1976 she met a former Secretary of the Navy, John Warner, who she decided would be a suitable future consort; indeed by Christmas she had married him and was soon thereafter campaigning for his seat in the Senate, which Warner eventually won in 1979 after the death in an air crash of the man who had defeated him in an election a few months earlier.

The role of the political wife, while new to Liz, was not altogether outside her training or background: a lesser movie talent, the actress Nancy Davis, had after all managed to get Ronald Reagan into the White House, and much of the personal-appearance work for which Taylor had been trained all those years ago by Metro now came back to her on the Senate trail. Warner was by general recognition good-looking and well capable of minor political office, if a little uninspired, and although some of Taylor's livelier Hollywood and New York friends found him conversationally dead, there was no doubt that after the tumult of the Burton years he had something altogether different, more peaceful and respectable to offer, not least a two-thousand acre farm in Virginia from where he was planning his Senate campaign.

If she gave him publicity and stardom and all the photo-opportunities he would not have enjoyed in an otherwise backwoods campaign, he gave her a kind of security and a valid reason for not having to tout around for any more movies. It also seemed reassuring that he was a millionaire from his first marriage into the Mellon family, and that he had his own Washington law practice: maybe at forty-four she really could go into the retirement that she had so long threatened or promised.

For the two years after her marriage to Warner, Liz did very little but campaign for him and put on weight: up to 180 pounds, so that middle-aged matrons all over Virginia noted that they had always wanted to look like Elizabeth Taylor and now alas they did. Never at her best in public appearances, she nevertheless managed to shake so many electors' hands that for weeks her fingers had to be bandaged, and though the eighteen-thousand-mile campaign trail grew more than a little wearisome she only once broke away from it, going to Vienna for Hal Prince to play Desiree Armfeldt in his film of Sondheim's *A Little Night Music*.

This was an elegant, stylish and starry picture (the cast included Diana Rigg and Hermione Gingold) that totally failed to catch the magic of the original stage musical, not least because Liz's singing of *Send in the Clowns* had to be heard not to be believed. It proved to be another, though mercifully the last, in the run of box-office disasters that Taylor had been involved with at the rate of one or two a year since *Taming of the Shrew* back in 1967; so it was not perhaps surprising that she remained altogether unbankable except in upstate Virginia, where opinion was still divided about whether Warner stood to win or lose more votes by being everywhere seen with a high-profile but seven-times-married wife.

Taylor attacked her new role as Mrs Warner with all the energy that she had brought to the best of her screen work, but as the long Virginia months dragged on the more perceptive of her interviewers noticed a kind of regally

With Len Cariou in a disastrous film of the Stephen Sondheim musical *A Little Night Music* (1977).

glazed boredom overtaking her initial enthusiasm for the new life. The central problem was perhaps that Warner, for all his Kennedy looks, was never going to achieve anything more than a seat in the Senate, and then only on an extremely Conservative ticket which Liz, from a vaguely Hollywood-liberal background, found repressive, especially when he refused even to have the Equal Rights Amendment mentioned around the campaign trail. If she was going to be a political wife for the rest of her life, then it would need to be to a President or at the very least a Kissinger figure rather than this slightly pompous prospective Senator from the sticks. Indeed, no sooner had he lost on his first bid for power than she returned to Hollywood and a television movie, *Return*

Engagement, which cast her as a college professor falling in love with one of her students. Reviews were terrible, not least for her figure, and she swiftly returned to Virginia, where by now Warner was again campaigning for the seat which he had previously lost to Richard Obenshain, and which had now become vacant owing to Obenshain's sudden death.

After some more heavy stumping of the Virginia farming territory he finally got sent to the Capitol in January 1979, and after a much-copied photograph of Warner and the chesty Liz was seen on the front page of all local papers a disgruntled non-voter gave it as his opinion that the state had just elected the three biggest boobs in the country. But if Elizabeth had found the campaign trail boring, she found Washington worse; the life of a minor-state Senator was not exactly close to the levers of power, and when the chance came to head back to London for a film which looked at last as though it could give her a box-office hit after nearly fifteen years in the wilderness, she not surprisingly took it very rapidly indeed.

Agatha Christie's *The Mirror Crack'd* was a routine pin-brained Miss Marple whodunnit which the makers dressed up with an all-star cast (Angela Lansbury, Edward Fox, Geraldine Chaplin, Rock Hudson, Kim Novak, Tony Curtis) and then the added attraction of Novak and Taylor sending themselves up as a couple of feuding over-the-top actresses from the old Hollywood.

With her sixth and (thus far) last husband John Warner in 1978.

174

Though the dialogue here was not exactly Wildean in its
wit (Novak to Taylor: 'Chin up, darling, both of them';
Taylor to Novak: 'There are two things I've always
admired about you: your face') the film was actually very
valuable, not only at the box-office but also in re-
establishing Taylor as someone who could laugh at her
own image and whose movies did not always have to
disappear into a black hole of non-distribution.

Having done little else in the last two years but a rapid
television guest-appearance in *Victory at Entebbe* and
one or two personal-appearance specials to keep her name
alive, Liz had found on the *Mirror Crack'd* location,
surrounded by such old Hollywood friends and former co-
stars as Rock Hudson and Angela Lansbury, with whom
she'd started in *National Velvet* thirty-three years earlier,
that she really ached to get back to some acting work. Now
that Warner was at last elected and spending most of his
days and nights trying to convince the Virginia con-
stituents that he was a hard-working Senator and not
some old film star's husband having an easy Washington
ride, there was really no marriage to keep alive and her
career seemed once again the only route forward.

Neither the cinema nor television was showing any
signs of a contract, so Liz would have to rebuild that
career in the only arena she had never really entered: the
theatre. That meant Broadway, and essentially a company under her own management: it also meant finding a

suitable play. *Virginia Woolf* was perhaps the most obvious choice, but friends persuaded her that it might lead to unfavourable comparisons with the movie of fifteen years earlier. Casting around for another larger-than-life harridan role to suit her present physical and vocal shape, it didn't take too long to arrive at Regina Giddens, the demon killer of Lillian Hellman's 1939 classic of Deep Southern family treachery *The Little Foxes*. As sacred monsters go, Regina (played originally on stage by Tallulah Bankhead and in the movie by Bette Davis) is one of the most sacrosanct, and the trouble with Taylor was that she gave nothing more than a very small performance inside a very large costume. Nevertheless it was brave to open in Washington and then go straight on to Broadway and a long tour ending in London, where most other movie stars might have chosen the gentler option of a season in Los Angeles among friends rather than critical butchers.

By the time *Little Foxes* reached London, the Hellman melodrama dedicated to the notion that the family which decays together stays together was looking distinctly tacky in both setting and supporting cast. But the main problem was Taylor's breathtaking lack of any stage technique. In one-to-one confrontations, the kind that might have been filmed in close-up, she had a certain shaky authority, but in the general family scenes she tended to vanish, despite the fact that the rest of the cast then retreated upstage as if in the presence of minor Balkan royalty. All in all it was an evening for stargazing rather than stardom, but the reviews around America and even in London did little to deter her new-found enthusiasm for the theatre, and sadly also little to encourage her to go in search of a good drama coach. The woman whom Burton had once called 'a raucous, intellectual Ethel Merman' had recognized a flamboyant theatrical home but not the need to train for it, and around the time of her fiftieth birthday (celebrated during the London run of *Little Foxes* in 1982) it was perhaps a little late to be sending her back to theatre school for such techniques as voice projection and posture, none of which had ever much mattered when there were microphones and cutaway cameras around.

On Broadway as Regina Giddens in *The Little Foxes* (1981), the role created by Tallulah Bankhead and filmed by Bette Davis.

Still remarkably accident-prone (she played much of the London run of *Little Foxes* in a wheelchair after yet another stay in hospital for what was reckoned to be her thirty-second operation) Taylor nonetheless now set out to prove that old violet eyes was back, and back to stay. Like that great survivor of the Sondheim song in *Follies*, the show she always should have done somewhere and never did, good times and bum times she'd seen them all, and my dears she was still here.

Not always in the most distinguished of settings, it had to be said. Her first job back in America after the tour of *Little Foxes* was a guest-turn on *General Hospital*, an ABC soap opera whose star Tony Geary was frequently to be seen escorting her around town as rumours spread that the Warner marriage was now at an end. Sure enough, early in 1982 she announced a separation, with the most detailed explanation yet of why another divorce (her sixth) was now imminent: 'Being a Senator's wife is not easy, I wouldn't wish it on anyone. I really loved John and I wanted to be the best wife anyone ever had. I wanted this to be a lifelong run. I would have done anything: licked stamps, typed speeches, run errands, anything. Instead I was just sitting at home watching the boob tube. My life had no meaning or responsibility; work is John's life, his wife, his mistress, his family. There just didn't seem to be room for anything or anyone else.'

And so, at fifty, Taylor was at last on her own: the survivor of seven marriages to six husbands of whom only Warner, Burton and Fisher were by now alive, the star of over fifty movies and an increasing number of rapid television appearances, was setting out on a 1980s decade which would be the first in her life almost totally devoid of marital commitments of any kind. Quite what she planned to do in all the years stretching out from her fiftieth birthday was anybody's guess, principally hers: evidently there was no longer going to be any support system of studios or even husbands. She would have to go it alone, and as the last of the old Hollywood machine-made stars, she wasn't going to find it easy; on the other hand the attempt might well prove more interesting and variable than the doom and gloom of the later Burton years.

Both as it happened were now at the end of other marriages, and though even they had come to accept that a third reconciliation would be bordering on farce rather than romance, they did consent to a joint appearance on a Bob Hope television special, and even began talking about a possible *Private Lives* for Broadway in 1983. At this moment, Taylor was successfully suing a television company which had threatened to invade her privacy with a tele-drama based on her life and times; at the very least, as she had the grace not to remark, one would have expected a mini-series. But the ex-Burtons apparently saw nothing exploitative in a revival of Coward's comedy about two divorced people clambering back to each other over the wreckage of subsequent marriages; or if they did, they consoled themselves with the thought that it was they themselves who would be doing the exploitation at the box-office.

Only it didn't happen quite like that: *Private Lives* opened in Boston early in the new year to some of the worst reviews since Pearl Harbor, limped into New York with a change of director (though not alas of cast) and barely staggered on there into the summer. A once great light comedy had been turned into a dance of death, through which Burton sleepwalked in a deep trance while Taylor desperately tried to remember what she was supposed to be saying next. The backstage atmosphere was not much improved when Richard took advantage of one

of Elizabeth's many nights off from the show to fly to Vegas and marry his last wife, Sally Hay; and though the show continued to limp along at the box-office for a few more weeks, a subsequent tour was curtailed. This cannot have been bad news for them, since the pre-bookings on Broadway alone guaranteed them forty thousand pounds a week each until the notices and word of mouth caught up with the advance, but it was perhaps bad news for a particularly ghoulish kind of audience which now clustered around the stage door and even ran down the aisles during the performance, apparently eager to touch legendary figures who might not be around for very much longer. In Burton's case they were of course absolutely right: he was dead in barely a year.

Undeterred by reviews which in my case described her in *Private Lives* as almost achieving brief flashes of near-adequacy, Taylor went bashing on into another television movie (*Between Friends* with Carol Burnett), all the while denying that in retaliation for the Burton remarriage she was about to approach the altar with a Mexican lawyer called Victor Luna. But there was now a sense of despera-

tion about her professional future: in barely eight weeks on Broadway with *Private Lives* she had missed almost thirty performances, with everything from bronchitis to nervous exhaustion around the time of the Richard remarriage, and the insurance company was in for at least five hundred thousand dollars in refund claims. All plans to carry on the Taylor theatre season with such announced attractions as *Sweet Bird of Youth* (which would have been a vastly better idea than either *Private Lives* or *Little Foxes*, concerned as it is with an over-the-hill movie star) were now abandoned altogether, and Home Box Office even declined to tape *Private Lives*, on the grounds that Taylor's weight problem made it an unattractive television prospect.

When Elizabeth reappeared in the headlines six months later, it was with the not totally shocking announcement that she had been admitted to the Betty Ford clinic for those recovering from dependency on drugs and alcohol. By now a photograph of Liz at her most bloated had reached the cover of *Hollywood Babylon*, and her family convinced her the time had come for a drastic cure: 'I would start to say something and the thought from my brain just never reached my tongue.'

Seven gruelling weeks later she emerged thin, strong and in remarkably good shape: good enough to go straight into a television series called *Hotel* and a new affair with a New York businessman called Dennis Stein who now joined Victor Luna in a queue of escorts to whom Liz briefly considered marriage. However, armed with the Betty Ford philosophy of lone survival from within, she seemed at last to have reached the point in her life where she no longer needed to have much more than a secretary around to pick up the pieces. She also took understandable pride in being the first major celebrity to go into the Ford Clinic and then talk openly about its ability to cure, thereby carving an acceptable path for such later stars in there as Mary Tyler Moore and Liza Minnelli. What saved Taylor, she recalled, 'was a day in hospital when my children and my brother and Roddy McDowall all came to see me and told me that if I didn't get off the drugs and quickly I would die. So I realized I'd reached the bottom, and after that it wasn't too difficult to get off the drink as well, because I really knew that I didn't want to die. I think I must have had hollow legs: I could consume vast quantities of alcohol without feeling drunk, but all my organs finally said that's it, Bessie, all over. I felt unneeded and very unnecessary: the children were all grown and I just got terribly fat.'

Thin and fifty-five, and a grandmother six times over, Liz Taylor—The Sequel as friends were already calling her seemed by late 1987 to be starting out all over again. The actress only recently described as looking like the Wife of Bath after being run over by a Brink's truck suddenly now began to qualify for learned retrospectives at movie festivals as critics and audiences awoke with a start to the realization that in there somewhere, amid all the marriages and the junk movies and the headlines, was also a history of the post-war Hollywood film industry: in a total of fifty-four feature films she had worked with the likes of Huston and Minnelli and Cukor and Mankiewicz, managing all the while to live a life of equally high off-screen intensity. For a social history of Taylor's adopted USA, you have only to look at the way she was reflected on its movie screens across forty years.

True, the 1980s have seen a lot of minor television and no major movies. After playing one of the first of her great enemies, the gossip columnist Louella Parsons in a waspish small-screen biopic called *Malice in Wonderland*, Liz celebrated her new slim frame with appearances in a mini-series called *North and South* (about the Civil War) and *There Must Be a Pony*, before turning to her first-ever western, yet another television film called *Poker Alice* in which she plays a well-born lady who wins a brothel after a card-sharping victory over George Hamilton, the actor she demanded for a co-star in her last two television assignments and who had by now become her most constant and urbane escort, precisely the kind of suitor who might have been assigned to her by an MGM charm school back in about 1947.

These things do have a tendency to go around in circles, and it may well be that Taylor and Hamilton will eventually finish up as the last golden couple in the Hollywood or at any rate the video twilight; but along the way she has taken the time to branch out into a profitable line of perfume commercials and into an admirable political battle to get the American authorities to awaken to the fact that the AIDS virus, which killed her old friend and co-star Rock Hudson, is not an exclusively homosexual problem. The two projects are not as unconnected as it might have been thought: all her profits from the million-dollar perfume campaign will in fact go to the AIDS charities, to which in Taylor's view the rest of America was giving too little and too late.

By December 1987 there were reports that Hamilton had been ditched in favour of another old flame, the millionaire publisher Malcolm Forbes; but more importantly, there was the news that Liz was back at work on the wide screen for the first time in seven years. Franco Zeffirelli, her director on *The Taming of the Shrew* in the best of the Burton years, had tempted her back to Rome to play a Russian soprano in *Young Toscanini*, a film biography of the great conductor. Her character in the film was that of a diva having a difficult and tempestuous comeback after years away from the footlights.

But Liz was determined that in real life she was not to become another of those doomed Hollywood superstars whose returns are even more depressing than their departures. Indeed, to prove that Liz the Sequel was now in business, she even embarked on *Elizabeth Takes Off*, a diet-and-health book on the Jane Fonda model but interleaved with the occasional if tantalisingly brief glimmer of autobiography.

So Mother Courage in Sables hadn't elected to wrap it up quite yet: sadly however, none of Taylor's happy endings ever seem to last longer than the credit titles at the end of a movie. The Zeffirelli film was previewed at the 1988 Venice Film Festival to reviews marginally worse than usual, though Alexander Walker noted that she did at least look ravishing in a film which would probably please those more familiar with a chocolate box than an opera box.

Worse was still to come: just as the diet-and-health book began to climb the bestseller charts on both sides of the Atlantic, it was revealed that the author herself had retreated to the Betty Ford Clinic again, 'wracked with pain, alone and back on pills and the booze' as the *Sun* gleefully reported. But the real problem now was that the Taylor story had started to look like the worst kind of B movie as she lurched from clinic to comeback, with often only days in between. Apart from the AIDS benefits Liz had no real work, and that in the past had always been her salvation. Rumours persisted that she would star in a film version of Tennessee Williams's *Sweet Bird of Youth*, but those rumours have been around for the best part of twenty years without approaching any kind of reality; moreover the critical mauling given to the *Young Toscanini* venture had not encouraged too much other interest in her at the box-office.

Writers eager to see in her troubles a remake of the Judy Garland or Marilyn Monroe stories have never yet understood the essential difference. Taylor is both English and a fighter, an actress who could never quite accept the theory that the great American dream could always turn into a nightmare at the close. What separates her from the doomed superstars of an earlier generation is the simple belief that in the end you have to go on living, at whatever the cost.

Soon after the 1987 Cannes Film Festival, the President of France solemnly bestowed upon a somewhat amazed Taylor the ribbon of the Legion of Honour; but then again, that's what they've always given to great survivors. Good times and bum times, she's seen them all and she's still here.

Filmography

1   There's One Born Every Minute

DIRECTOR   Harold Young
SCENARIO   Original Story: Robert B. Hunt
PHOTOGRAPHY   John W. Boyle
EDITOR   Maurice Wright
CAST   Hugh Herbert, Peggy Moran, Tom Brown, Guy
  Kibbee, Catherine Doucet, Edgar Kennedy, Scott
  Jordan, Gus Schilling, Elizabeth Taylor, Charles
  Halton, Renie Riano, Alfalfa Switzer
RUNNING TIME   59 minutes
RELEASED   1942
PRODUCED BY Universal

2   Lassie Come Home

DIRECTOR   Fred M. Wilson
SCENARIO   Hugh Butler. From the novel by Eric
  Knight
PHOTOGRAPHY   Leonard Smith
EDITOR   Ben Lewis
CAST   Roddy McDowall, Donald Crisp, Edmund
  Gwenn, Dame May Whitty, Nigel Bruce, Elsa
  Lanchester, Elizabeth Taylor, J. Patrick O'Malley,
  Ben Webster, Alec Craig, John Rogers, Arthur
  Shields, Pal
RUNNING TIME   88 minutes
RELEASED   1943
PRODUCED BY MGM

3   Jane Eyre

DIRECTOR   Robert Stevenson
SCENARIO   Aldous Huxley, Robert Stevenson, John
  Houseman
PHOTOGRAPHY   George Barnes
EDITOR   Walter Thompson
CAST   Orson Welles, Joan Fontaine, Margaret
  O'Brien, Peggy Ann Garner, John Sutton, Sara
  Allgood, Henry Daniell, Agnes Moorehead, Aubrey
  Mather, Edith Barrett, Barbara Everest, Hillary
  Brooke, Ethel Griffies, Mae Marsh, Eily Malyon,
  Mary Forbes, Thomas London, John Abbott,
  Ronald Harris, Charles Irwin, Elizabeth Taylor
RUNNING TIME   96 minutes
RELEASED   1943
PRODUCED BY 20th Century Fox

4   The White Cliffs of Dover

DIRECTOR   Clarence Brown
SCENARIO   Claudine West, Jan Lustig, George
  Froeschel. Based on the poem, 'The White Cliffs of
  Dover' by Alice Duer Miller. Additional poetry:
  Robert Nathan
PHOTOGRAPHY   George Folsey
EDITOR   Robert J. Kern
CAST   Irene Dunne, Alan Marshall, Frank Morgan,
  Dame May Whitty, C. Audrey Smith, Gladys
  Cooper, Isobel Elsom, Elizabeth Taylor, Roddy
  McDowall, Peter Lawford, Van Johnson, John
  Warburton, Jill Esmond, Brenda Forbes, Norma
  Varden, June Lockhart
RUNNING TIME   126 minutes
RELEASED   1944
PRODUCED BY MGM

5   National Velvet

DIRECTOR   Clarence Brown
SCENARIO   Theodore Reeves, Helen Deutsch. Based on
  the novel by Enid Bagnold
PHOTOGRAPHY   Leonard Smith
EDITOR   Robert J. Kern
CAST   Mickey Rooney, Donald Crisp, Elizabeth
  Taylor, Anne Revere, Angela Lansbury, Juanita
  Quigley, Jack Jenkins, Reginald Owen, Terry
  Kilburn, Alec Craig, Eugene Loring, Norma
  Varden, Arthur Shields, Dennis Hoey, Aubrey
  Mather, Frederick Warlock, Arthur Treacher
RUNNING TIME   125 minutes
RELEASED   1944
PRODUCED BY MGM

6   Courage of Lassie

DIRECTOR   Fred Wilcox
SCENARIO   Lionel Hauser
PHOTOGRAPHY   Leonard Smith
EDITOR   Conrad A. Nervig
CAST   Elizabeth Taylor, Frank Morgan, Tom Drake,
  Selena Royle, Harry Davenport, George Cleveland,
  Catherine McLeod, Morris Ankrum, Arthur Walsh,
  Mitchell Lewis, Jane Green, David Holt, William
  Lewin, Minor Watson, Windy Cook, Donald Curtis,
  Clancy Cooper, Lassie
RUNNING TIME   93 minutes
RELEASED   1946
PRODUCED BY MGM

7   Cynthia

DIRECTOR   Robert Z. Leonard
SCENARIO   Harold Buchman, Charles Kaufman. Based
  on the play, *The Rich Full Life*, by Vina Delmar
PHOTOGRAPHY   Charles Schoenbaum

EDITOR   Irvine Warburton
CAST   Elizabeth Taylor, George Murphy, S.Z. Sakall, Mary Astor, Gene Lockhart, Spring Byington, James Lydon, Scotty Beckett, Carol Brannan, Anna Q. Nilsson, Morris Ankrum, Kathleen Howard, Shirley Johns, Barbara Challis, Harlan Briggs, Will Wright
RUNNING TIME   98 minutes
RELEASED   1947
PRODUCED BY MGM

8   Life With Father

DIRECTOR   Michael Curtiz
SCENARIO   Donald Ogden Stewart. From the play by Howard Lindsay and Russell Crouse
PHOTOGRAPHY   Peverell Marley, William V. Skall
EDITOR   George Amy
CAST   William Powell, Irene Dunne, Elizabeth Taylor, Edmund Gwenn, ZaSu Pitts, Jimmy Lydon, Emma Dunn, Moroni Olsen, Elizabeth Risdon, Derek Scott, Johnny Calkins, Martin Milner, Heather Wilde, Monte Blue, Mary Field, Queenie Leonard, Clara Blandick, Frank Elliott
RUNNING TIME   118 minutes
RELEASED   1947
PRODUCED BY Warner Bros.

9   A Date with Judy

DIRECTOR   Richard Thorpe
SCENARIO   Dorothy Cooper, Dorothy Kingsley. Based on the characters created by Aleen Leslie
PHOTOGRAPHY   Robert Surtees
EDITOR   Harold F. Kress
CAST   Wallace Beery, Jane Powell, Elizabeth Taylor, Carmen Miranda, Xavier Cugat, Robert Stack, Leon Ames, Selena Royle, Scotty Beckett, George Cleveland, Lloyd Corrigan, Clinton Sundberg, Jean McLaren
RUNNING TIME   113 minutes
RELEASED   1948
PRODUCED BY MGM

10   Julia Misbehaves

DIRECTOR   Jack Conway
SCENARIO   William Ludwig, Harry Ruskin, Arthur Wimperis. Adaptation: Gina Kaus, Monckton Hoffe. Based on the novel, The Nutmeg Tree, by Margery Sharp
PHOTOGRAPHY   Joseph Ruttenberg
EDITOR   John Dunning
CAST   Greer Garson, Walter Pidgeon, Peter Lawford, Elizabeth Taylor, Cesar Romero, Lucile Watson, Nigel Bruce, Mary Boland, Reginald Owen, Henry Stephenson, Aubrey Mather, Fritz Feld, Phyllis Morris, Veda Ann Borg
RUNNING TIME   99 minutes
RELEASED   1948
PRODUCED BY MGM

11   Little Women

DIRECTOR   Mervin LeRoy
SCENARIO   Andrew Solt, Sarah Y. Mason, Victor Heerman. Based on the novel by Louisa May Alcott. Adaptation: Sally Benson
PHOTOGRAPHY   Robert Planck, Charles Schoenbaum
EDITOR   Ralph Winters
CAST   June Allyson, Peter Lawford, Margaret O'Brien, Elizabeth Taylor, Janet Leigh, Rossano Brazzi, Mary Astor, Lucile Watson, Sir C. Aubrey Smith, Elizabeth Patterson, Leon Ames, Harry Davenport, Richard Stapley, Connie Gilchrist, Ellen Corby
RUNNING TIME   87 minutes
RELEASED   1949
PRODUCED BY MGM

12   The Big Hangover

DIRECTOR   Norman Krasna
SCENARIO   Norman Krasna
PHOTOGRAPHY   George Folsey
EDITOR   Frederick Y. Smith
CAST   Van Johnson, Elizabeth Taylor, Percy Waram, Fay Holden, Edgar Buchanan, Selena Royle, Gene Lockhart, Leon Ames, Rosemary DeCamp, Philip Ahn, Pierre Watkin, Russell Hicks, Gordon Richards, Kathleen Lockhart
RUNNING TIME   82 minutes
RELEASED   1949
PRODUCED BY MGM

13   Conspirator

DIRECTOR   Victor Saville
SCENARIO   Sally Benson. Adaptation: Sally Benson, Gerald Fairlie. Based on the novel by Humphrey Slater
PHOTOGRAPHY   F. A. Young
EDITOR   Frank Clarke
CAST   Robert Taylor, Elizabeth Taylor, Robert Fleming, Harold Warrender, Honor Blackman, Marjorie Fielding, Thora Hird, Wilfred Hyde-White, Marie Ney, Jack Allen, Cicely Paget-Bowman, Karel Stepanek, Nicholas Bruce, Cyril Smith
RUNNING TIME   87 minutes
RELEASED   1949
PRODUCED BY Arthur Hornblower Jr

14   Father of the Bride

DIRECTOR   Vincente Minnelli
SCENARIO   Frances Goodrich, Albert Hackett. Based on the novel by Edward Streeter
PHOTOGRAPHY   John Alton
EDITOR   Ferris Webster
CAST   Spencer Tracy, Joan Bennett, Elizabeth Taylor, Don Taylor, Billie Burke, Leo G. Carroll, Moroni

Olsen, Melville Cooper, Taylor Holmes, Paul
Harvey, Frank Orth, Rusty Tamblyn, Tom Irish,
Marietta Canty, Willard Waterman, Nancy
Valentine, Mary Jane Smith, Jacqueline Duval, Fay
Baker, Frank Myers
RUNNING TIME 93 minutes
RELEASED 1950
PRODUCED BY MGM

15   Father's Little Dividend

DIRECTOR Vincente Minnelli
SCENARIO Albert Hackett, Frances Goodrich. Based
on characters created by Edward Streeter in his
book, *Father of the Bride*
PHOTOGRAPHY John Alton
EDITOR Ferris Webster
CAST Spencer Tracy, Joan Bennett, Elizabeth Taylor,
Don Taylor, Billie Burke, Maroni Olsen, Richard
Roper, Marietta Canty, Rusty Tamblyn, Tom Irish,
Hayden Rorke, Paul Harvey
RUNNING TIME 82 minutes
RELEASED 1951
PRODUCED BY MGM

16   A Place in the Sun

DIRECTOR George Stevens
SCENARIO Michael Wilson, Harry Brown. Based on
the novel, *An American Tragedy*, by Theodore
Dreiser, and the stage adaptation by Patrick
Kearney
PHOTOGRAPHY William C. Mellor
EDITOR William Hornbeck
CAST Montgomery Clift, Elizabeth Taylor, Shelly
Winters, Anne Revere, Keefe Brasselle, Fred Clark,
Raymond Burr, Herbert Heyes, Shepperd
Strudwick, Frieda Inescort, Kathryn Givney,
Walter Sande, Ted de Corsia, John Ridgely, Lois
Chartrand, William B. Murphy, Douglas Spencer,
Charles Dayton, Paul Frees
RUNNING TIME 122 minutes
RELEASED 1951
PRODUCED BY Paramount

17   Callaway Went Thataway

DIRECTOR Norman Panama, Melvin Frank
SCENARIO Norman Panama, Melvin Frank
PHOTOGRAPHY Ray June
EDITOR Cotton Warburton
CAST Fred MacMurray, Dorothy McGuire, Howard
Keel, Jesse White, Fay Roope, Natalie Schafer,
Douglas Kennedy, Elisabeth Fraser, Johnny
Indrisano, Stan Freberg, Don Haggerty, June
Allyson, Clark Gable, Dick Powell, Elizabeth
Taylor, Esther Williams
RUNNING TIME 81 minutes
RELEASED 1951
PRODUCED BY MGM

18   Love Is Better Than Ever
(G.B. title: The Light Fantastic)

DIRECTOR Stanley Donen
SCENARIO Ruth Brooks Flippen
PHOTOGRAPHY Harold Rosson
EDITOR George Boemler
CAST Larry Parks, Elizabeth Taylor, Josephine
Hutchinson, Tom Tully, Ann Doran, Elinor
Donahue, Kathleen Freeman, Doreen McCann,
Alex Gerry, Dick Wessel
RUNNING TIME 81 minutes
RELEASED 1952
PRODUCED BY MGM

19   Ivanhoe

DIRECTOR Richard Thorpe
SCENARIO Noel Langley. Adaptation: Aeneas
MacKenzie. From the novel by Sir Walter Scott
PHOTOGRAPHY F. A. Young
EDITOR Frank Clarke
CAST Robert Taylor, Elizabeth Taylor, Joan
Fontaine, George Sanders, Emlyn Williams, Guy
Rolfe, Robert Douglas, Finlay Currie, Felix Aylmer,
Carl Jaffe, Norman Wooland, Basil Sydney, Harold
Warrender, Patrick Holt, Roderick Lovell,
Sebastian Cabot, John Ruddock, Michael Brennan,
Valentine Dyall, Lionel Harris
RUNNING TIME 106 minutes
RELEASED 1952
PRODUCED BY MGM

20   The Girl Who Had Everything

DIRECTOR Richard Thorpe
SCENARIO Art Cohn. Based on *A Free Soul* by Adela
Rogers St Johns
PHOTOGRAPHY Paul Vogel
EDITOR Ben Lewis
CAST Elizabeth Taylor, Fernando Lamas, William
Powell, Gig Young, James Whitmore, Robert
Burton, William Walker
RUNNING TIME 69 minutes
RELEASED 1953
PRODUCED BY MGM

21   Rhapsody

DIRECTOR Charles Vidor
SCENARIO Fay and Michael Kanin. Adaptation: Ruth
and Agustus Goetz. Based on the novel, *Maurice
Guest*, by Henry Handel Richardson
PHOTOGRAPHY Robert Planck
EDITOR John Dunning
CAST Elizabeth Taylor, Vittorio Gassman, John
Ericson, Louis Calhern, Michael Chekhov, Barbara
Bates, Richard Hageman, Richard Lupino, Celia
Lovsky, Stuart Whitman, Madge Blake, Jack
Raine, Brigit Nielsen, Jacqueline Duval, Norma
Nevens

RUNNING TIME   115 minutes
RELEASED 1954
PRODUCED BY MGM

22   Elephant Walk

DIRECTOR   William Dieterle
SCENARIO   John Lee Mahin. Based on the novel by Robert Standish
PHOTOGRAPHY   Loyal Griggs
EDITOR   George Tomasini
CAST   Elizabeth Taylor, Dana Andrews, Peter Finch, Abraham Sofaer, Abner Biberman, Noel Drayton, Rosalind Ivan, Barry Bernard, Philip Tonge, Edward Ashley, Leo Britt, Mylee Haulani, The Madhyma Lanka Mandala Dancers
RUNNING TIME   103 minutes
RELEASED   1954
PRODUCED BY Paramount

23   Beau Brummell

DIRECTOR   Curtis Bernhardt
SCENARIO   Karl Tunberg. Based on the play by Clyde Fitch
PHOTOGRAPHY   Oswald Morris
EDITOR   Frank Clarke
CAST   Stewart Granger, Elizabeth Taylor, Peter Ustinov, Robert Morley, James Donald, James Hayter, Rosemary Harris, Paul Rogers, Noel Willman, Peter Dyneley, Charles Carson, Ernest Clark, Peter Bull, Mark Dignam, Desmond Roberts, David Horne, Ralph Truman, Elwyn Brook-Jones, George De Warfaz, Henry Oscar, Harold Kasket
RUNNING TIME   111 minutes
RELEASED   1954
PRODUCED BY MGM

24   The Last Time I Saw Paris

DIRECTOR   Richard Brooks
SCENARIO   Julius J. and Philip G. Epstein and Richard Brooks. Based on a story by F. Scott Fitzgerald
PHOTOGRAPHY   Joseph Ruttenberg
EDITOR   John Dunning
CAST   Elizabeth Taylor, Van Johnson, Walter Pidgeon, Donna Reed, Eva Gabor, Kurt Kasznar, George Dolenz, Roger Moore, Sandy Descher, Celia Lovsky, Peter Leeds, John Doucette, Odette
RUNNING TIME   116 minutes
RELEASED   1954
PRODUCED BY MGM

25   Giant

DIRECTOR   George Stevens
SCENARIO   Fred Guiol, Ivan Moffat. From the novel by Edna Ferber
PHOTOGRAPHY   William C. Mellor

EDITOR   William Hornbeck
CAST   Elizabeth Taylor, Rock Hudson, James Dean, Carroll Baker, Jane Withers, Chill Wills, Mercedes McCambridge, Sal Mineo, Dennis Hopper, Judith Evelyn, Paul Fix, Rodney Taylor, Earl Holliman, Robert Nichols, Alexander Scourby, Fran Bennett, Charles Watts, Elsa Cardenas, Carolyn Craig, Monte Hale
RUNNING TIME   198 minutes
RELEASED   1956
PRODUCED BY Warner Bros.

26   Raintree County

DIRECTOR   Edward Dmytryk
SCENARIO   Millard Kaufman. Based on the novel by Ross Lockridge Jr
PHOTOGRAPHY   Robert Surtees
EDITOR   John Dunning
CAST   Montgomery Clift, Elizabeth Taylor, Eva Marie Saint, Nigel Patrick, Lee Marvin, Rod Taylor, Agnes Moorehead, Walter Abel, Jarma Lewis, Tom Drake, Rhys Williams, Russell Collins, DeForrest Kelley
RUNNING TIME   166 minutes
RELEASED   1957
PRODUCED BY MGM

27   Cat on a Hot Tin Roof

DIRECTOR   Richard Brooks
SCENARIO   Richard Brooks, James Poe. Based on the play by Tennessee Williams
PHOTOGRAPHY   William Daniels
EDITOR   Ferris Webster
CAST   Elizabeth Taylor, Paul Newman, Burl Ives, Jack Carson, Judith Anderson, Madeleine Sherwood, Larry Gates, Vaughn Taylor, Patty Ann Gerrity, Rusty Stevens, Hugh Corcoran, Deborah Miller, Brian Corcoran, Vince Townsend Jr, Zelda Cleaver
RUNNING TIME   108 minutes
RELEASED   1958
PRODUCED BY MGM

28   Suddenly Last Summer

DIRECTOR   Joseph L. Mankiewicz
SCENARIO   Gore Vidal, Tennessee Williams. Adapted from the play by Tennessee Williams
PHOTOGRAPHY   Jack Hildyard
EDITOR   Thomas G. Stanford
CAST   Elizabeth Taylor, Katharine Hepburn, Montgomery Clift, Albert Dekker, Mercedes McCambridge, Gary Raymond, Mavis Villiers, Patricia Marmont, Joan Young, Maria Britneva, Sheila Robbins, David Cameron
RUNNING TIME   114 minutes
RELEASED   1959
PRODUCED BY Horizon

29 Scent of Mystery
(G.B. title: Holiday in Spain)

DIRECTOR Jack Cardiff
SCENARIO William Roos. Based on an original story
  by Kelly Roos
PHOTOGRAPHY John Von Kotze
EDITOR James Newcom
CAST Denholm Elliott, Peter Lorre, Beverly Bentley,
  Paul Lukas, Liam Redmond, Leo McKern, Peter
  Arne, Diana Dors, Mary Laura Wood, Judith
  Furse, Maurice Marsac, Michael Trubshawe, Juan
  Olaguivel, Billie Miller, Elizabeth Taylor
RUNNING TIME 125 minutes
RELEASED 1960
PRODUCED BY Michael Todd Jr

30 Butterfield 8

DIRECTOR Daniel Mann
SCENARIO Charles Schnee, John Michael Hayes.
  Based on the novel by John O'Hara
PHOTOGRAPHY Joseph Ruttenberg, Charles Harten
EDITOR Ralph E. Winters
CAST Elizabeth Taylor, Laurence Harvey, Eddie
  Fisher, Dina Merrill, Mildred Dunnock, Betty Field,
  Jeffrey Lynn, Kay Medford, Susan Oliver, George
  Voskovec, Virginia Downing, Carmen Matthews,
  Whitfield Connor
RUNNING TIME 109 minutes
RELEASED 1960
PRODUCED BY MGM/Apton – Linebrook

31 Cleopatra

DIRECTOR Joseph L. Mankiewicz
SCENARIO Joseph L. Mankiewicz, Ranald
  MacDougall, Sidney Buchman. Based upon
  histories by Plutarch, Suetonius, Appian, other
  ancient sources, and *The Life and Times of
  Cleopatra* by C. M. Francero
PHOTOGRAPHY Leon Shamroy
EDITOR Dorothy Spencer
CAST Elizabeth Taylor, Richard Burton, Rex
  Harrison, Pamela Brown, George Cole, Hume
  Cronyn, Cesare Danova, Kenneth Haigh, Andrew
  Keir, Martin Landau, Roddy McDowall, Robert
  Stephens, Francesca Annis, Gregoire Aslan, Martin
  Benson, Herbert Berghof, John Cairney, Jacqui
  Chan, Isabelle Cooley, John Duocette, Andrew
  Faulds, Michael Gwynne, Michael Hordern, John
  Hoyt, Marne Maitland, Carrol O'Connor, Richard
  O'Sullivan, Gwen Watford, Douglas Wilmer, Finlay
  Currie, Marina Berti, John Karlsen, Loris Loddi,
  Del Russell, Kenneth Nash, Jean Marsh, Gin Mart,
  Furio Meniconi, John Valva, Laurence Naismith,
  John Alderson, Peter Foster
RUNNING TIME 243 minutes
RELEASED 1963
PRODUCED BY 20th Century-Fox

32 The VIPs

DIRECTOR Anthony Asquith
SCENARIO Terence Rattigan
PHOTOGRAPHY Jack Hildyard
EDITOR Frank Clarke
CAST Elizabeth Taylor, Richard Burton, Louis
  Jordan, Elsa Martinelli, Margaret Rutherford,
  Maggie Smith, Rod Taylor, Orson Welles, Linda
  Christian, Dennis Price, Richard Wattis, David
  Frost, Ronald Fraser, Robert Coote, Michael
  Hordern, Martin Miller, Lance Percival, Joan
  Benham, Peter Sallis, Stringer Davis, Clifton Jones,
  Moyra Fraser
RUNNING TIME 119 minutes
RELEASED 1963
PRODUCED BY MGM

33 The Sandpiper

DIRECTOR Vincente Minnelli
SCENARIO Dalton Trumbo, Michael Wilson.
  Adaptation: Irene and Louis Kamp. Story: Martin
  Ransohoff
PHOTOGRAPHY Milton Krasner
EDITOR David Bretherton
CAST Elizabeth Taylor, Richard Burton, Eva Marie
  Saint, Charles Bronson, Robert Webber, James
  Edwards, Torin Thatcher, Tom Drake, Doug
  Henderson, Morgan Mason
RUNNING TIME 116 minutes
RELEASED 1965
PRODUCED BY MGM/Filmway

34 Who's Afraid of Virginia Woolf?

DIRECTOR Mike Nichols
SCENARIO Ernest Lehman. From the play by Edward
  Albee
PHOTOGRAPHY Haskell Wexler
EDITOR Sam O'Steen
CAST Elizabeth Taylor, Richard Burton, George
  Segal, Sandy Dennis
RUNNING TIME 130 minutes
RELEASED 1966
PRODUCED BY Warner Bros.

35 The Taming of the Shrew

DIRECTOR Franco Zeffirelli
SCENARIO Paul Dehn, Suso Cecchi D'Amico, Franco
  Zeffirelli (with acknowledgements to William
  Shakespeare)
PHOTOGRAPHY Oswald Morris
EDITOR Peter Taylor
CAST Elizabeth Taylor, Richard Burton, Cyril
  Cusack, Michael Hordern, Alfred Lynch, Alan
  Webb, Victor Spinetti, Roy Holder, Mark Dignam,
  Bice Valori, Natasha Pyne, Michael York,
  Giancarlo Cobelli, Vernon Dobtcheff, Ken Parry,
  Anthony Gardner

RUNNING TIME 122 minutes
RELEASED 1967
PRODUCED BY Columbia

36 Doctor Faustus

DIRECTOR Richard Burton, Nevill Coghill
SCENARIO Nevill Coghill. Based on the play, *The Tragic History of Doctor Faustus*, by Christopher Marlowe
PHOTOGRAPHY Gabor Pogany
EDITOR John Shirley
CAST Richard Burton, Elizabeth Taylor, Andreas Teuber, Elizabeth O'Donovan, Ian Marter, Jeremy Eccles, David McIntosh, Ram Chopra, Richard Carwardine, Adrian Benjamin, Richard Heffer, Hugh Williams, Gwydion Thomas, Nicholas Loukes, Richard Durden-Smith, Patrick Barwise, Jeremy Chandler, Angus McIntosh, Ambrose Coghill, Anthony Kaufmann, Julian Wontner, Richard Harrison, Nevill Coghill, Michael Menaugh, John Sandbach, Sebastian Walker, R. Peverello, Maria Aitken, Valerie James, Bridget Coghill, Petronella Pulsford, Susan Watson, Jacqueline Harvey, Sheila Dawson, Carolyn Bennitt, Jane Wilford
RUNNING TIME 93 minutes
RELEASED 1967
PRODUCED BY Columbia (an Oxford University Screen Production)

37 Reflections in a Golden Eye

DIRECTOR John Huston
SCENARIO Chapman Mortimer, Gladys Hill. Based on the novel by Carson McCullers
PHOTOGRAPHY Aldo Tonti
EDITOR Russell Lloyd
CAST Elizabeth Taylor, Marlon Brando, Brian Keith, Julie Harris, Robert Forster, Zorro David, Gordon Mitchell, Irvin Dugan, Fay Sparks
RUNNING TIME 109 minutes
RELEASED 1967
PRODUCED BY Warner Bros – Seven Arts

38 The Comedians

DIRECTOR Peter Glenville
SCENARIO Graham Greene (from his novel)
PHOTOGRAPHY Henri Decae
EDITOR Francoise Javet
CAST Richard Burton, Elizabeth Taylor, Alec Guinness, Peter Ustinov, Paul Ford, Lillian Gish, George Stanford Brown, Roscoe Lee Browne, Gloria Foster, James Earl Jones, Zaeks Mokae, Douta Seck, Raymont St Jacques, Cicely Tyson
RUNNING TIME 160 minutes
RELEASED 1967
PRODUCED MGM

39 Boom!

DIRECTOR Joseph Losey
SCENARIO Tennessee Williams, based on his play *The Milk Train Doesn't Stop Here Any More*
PHOTOGRAPHY Douglas Slocombe
EDITOR Reginald Back
CAST Elizabeth Taylor, Richard Burton, Noël Coward, Joanna Shimkus, Michael Dunn, Romolo Valli, Fernando Piazza, Veronica Wells, Howard Taylor
RUNNING TIME 110 minutes
RELEASED 1968
PRODUCED BY Universal

40 Secret Ceremony

DIRECTOR Joseph Losey
SCENARIO George Tabori. Based on a short story by Marco Denevi
PHOTOGRAPHY Gerald Fisher
EDITOR Reginald Beck
CAST Elizabeth Taylor, Mia Farrow, Robert Mitchum, Peggy Ashcroft, Pamela Brown
RUNNING TIME 109 minutes
RELEASED 1968 GB
PRODUCED BY Universal

41 The Only Game in Town

DIRECTOR George Stevens
SCENARIO Frank D. Gilroy (based on his play)
PHOTOGRAPHY Henri Decae
EDITOR John W. Holmes, William Sands, Pat Shade
CAST Elizabeth Taylor, Warren Beatty, Charles Braswell, Hank Henry
RUNNING TIME 113 minutes
RELEASED 1969
PRODUCED BY 20th Century-Fox

42 Under Milk Wood

DIRECTOR Andrew Sinclair
SCENARIO Andrew Sinclair. From the verse drama by Dylan Thomas
PHOTOGRAPHY Bob Huke
EDITOR Willy Kemplen
CAST Richard Burton, Elizabeth Taylor, Peter O'Toole, Glynis Johns, Vivien Merchant, Sian Phillips, Victor Spinetti, Ryan Davies, Angharad Rees, Ray Smith
RUNNING TIME 90 minutes
RELEASED 1971

43 Zee & Co., (U.S. title: X, Y & Zee)

DIRECTOR Brian Hutton
SCENARIO Edna O'Brien
PHOTOGRAPHY Billy Williams
EDITOR Jim Clark
CAST Elizabeth Taylor, Michael Caine, Susannah

York, Margaret Leighton, John Standing, Mary Larkin, Michael Cashman, Gino Melvazzi, Julian West, Hilary West
RUNNING TIME 110 minutes
RELEASED 1971
PRODUCED BY Columbia

44 Hammersmith Is Out

DIRECTOR Peter Ustinov
SCENARIO Stanford Whitmore
PHOTOGRAPHY Richard H. Kline
EDITOR David Blewitt
CAST Elizabeth Taylor, Richard Burton, Peter Ustinov, Beau Bridges, Leon Ames, Leon Akin, John Schuck, Carl Doun, George Raft, Marjorie Eaton, Lisa Jak, Linda Gaye Scott, Mel Berger, Anthony Holland, Brook Williams, Jose Espnoza
RUNNING TIME 108 minutes
RELEASED 1972
PRODUCED BY J. Cornelius Crean Films

45 Divorce His, Divorce Hers*

DIRECTOR Waris Hussein
SCENARIO John Hopkins
PHOTOGRAPHY Ernest Wild, Gabor Pogany
EDITOR John Bloom
CAST Richard Burton, Elizabeth Taylor, Carrie Nye, Barry Foster, Gabriele Ferzetti, Daniela Surina, Thomas Baptiste, Ronald Radd, Rudolph Walker, Mark Colleano, Rossalyn Landor, Eva Griffith, Marietta Schupp
RUNNING TIME 180 minutes
RELEASED 1973
PRODUCED BY ABC-TV

46 Night Watch

DIRECTOR Brian Hutton
SCENARIO Tony Williamson. Additional dialogue Evan Jones. Based upon the play by Lucille , Fletcher
PHOTOGRAPHY Billy Williams
EDITOR John Jympson
CAST Elizabeth Taylor, Laurence Harvey, Billie Whitelaw, Robert Lang, Tony Britton, Bill Dean, Michael D. Walker, Rosario Serrano, Pauline Jameson, Linda Hayden, Kevin Colson, Laon Maybanke
RUNNING TIME 99 minutes
RELEASED 1973
PRODUCED BY Avco Embassy

47 Ash Wednesday

DIRECTOR Larry Peerce
SCENARIO Jean-Claude Tramont
PHOTOGRAPHY Ennio Guarnieri
EDITOR Marion Rothman
CAST Elizabeth Taylor, Henry Fonda, Helmut

Berger, Keith Baxter, Maurice Teynac, Margaret Blye, Dino Mele, Carlo Puri, Jill Pratt, Andrea Esterhazy, Irina Wassilchikoff, Jose de Bega, Dina Sassoli, Muki Windisch-Graetz, Nadia Stancioff, Raymond Vignale, Jack Kepp, Piero Baccante, Gianni Rossi, Kathy Heinsieck, Rodolfo Lodi, Samantha Starr, Monique Van Vooren, Henning Schlüeter
RUNNING TIME 99 minutes
RELEASED 1973
PRODUCED BY Paramount

48 That's Entertainment!

DIRECTOR Jack Haley Jr
SCENARIO Jack Haley Jr
PHOTOGRAPHY Gene Polito, Ernest Laszlo, Russel Metty, Ennio Guarnieri, Allen Green
EDITOR Bud Friedgen, David E. Blewitt
CAST Fred Astaire, Bing Crosby, Gene Kelly, Peter Lawford, Liza Minnelli, Donald O'Connor, Debbie Reynolds, Mickey Rooney, Frank Sinatra, James Stewart, Elizabeth Taylor
RUNNING TIME 132 minutes
RELEASED 1974
PRODUCED BY MGM

49 Identikit (G.B. title: The Driver's Seat)

DIRECTOR Giuseppe Patroni-Griffi
SCENARIO Muriel Spark (from her novella), Raffaele La Capria, Giuseppe Patroni-Griffi
PHOTOGRAPHY Bittorio Storaro
CAST Elizabeth Taylor, Ian Bannen, Guido Mannaro, Mona Washbourne, Maxence Mailfort
RUNNING TIME 105 minutes
RELEASED 1974
PRODUCED BY Avco Embassy

50 The Blue Bird

DIRECTOR George Cukor
SCENARIO Hugh Whitemore and Alfred Hayes. Russian version of screenplay Alexei Kapler
PHOTOGRAPHY Ionas Gritzus and Freddie Young
CAST Elizabeth Taylor, Jane Fonda, Cicely Tyson, Ava Gardner, Todd Lockinland, Patsy Kensit, Will Geer, Mona Washbourne, Robert Morley, Harry Andrews, James Coco, Richard Pearson, Nadejda Pavlova, Margareta Terechova, Oleg Popov, Georgi Vitzin, Leonid Nevedomsky, Valentina Ganilaee Ganibalova, Yevgeny Scherbakov
RUNNING TIME 100 minutes
RELEASED 1976
PRODUCED BY 20th Century-Fox

51 Victory at Entebbe

DIRECTOR Marvin J. Chomsky
SCENARIO Ernest Kinoy
PHOTOGRAPHY James Kilgore

EDITOR Jim McElroy and Mike Gavaldon
CAST Helmut Berger, Theodore Bikel, Linda Blair, Kirk Douglas, Richard Dreyfuss, Stefan Gierasch, David Groh, Julius Harris (replaced Godfrey Cambridge who died during production), Helen Hayes, Anthony Hopkins, Burt Lancaster, Christian Marquand, Elizabeth Taylor, Jessica Walter, Harris Yulin, Allan Miller, Bibi Besch
RUNNING TIME 119 minutes
RELEASED 1976
PRODUCED BY David L. Wolper Production

52   A Little Night Music

DIRECTOR Harold Prince
SCENARIO Hugh Wheeler
PHOTOGRAPHY Arthur Ibbetson BSc
EDITOR John Jympson
CAST Elizabeth Taylor, Diana Rigg, Len Cariou, Lesley-Ann Down, Hermione Gingold, Laurence Guittard, Christopher Guard, Chloe Franks, Heinz Marecek, Lesley Dunlop, Jonathan Tunick, Herbert Tscheppe, Rudolf Schrympf
RUNNING TIME 125 minutes
RELEASED 1977
PRODUCED BY A New World Picture

53   Return Engagement*

DIRECTOR Joseph Hardy
SCENARIO James Prideaux
PHOTOGRAPHY Tom Schamp
CAST Elizabeth Taylor, Joseph Bottoms, Peter Donat, Allyn Ann McLerie, James Ray
RUNNING TIME 89 minutes
RELEASED November 17 1978
PRODUCED BY NBC-TV

54   Winter Kills

DIRECTOR William Richert
SCENARIO William Richert. Based on a book by Richard Condon
PHOTOGRAPHY Vilmos Zsigmond
EDITOR David Bretherton
CAST Jeff Bridges, John Huston, Anthony Perkins, Eli Wallach, Sterling Hayden, Dorothy Malone, Tomas Milian, Belinda Bauer, Ralph Meeker, Toshiro Mifune, Richard Boone, David Spielberg, Brad Dexter, Michael Thoma, Elizabeth Taylor
RUNNING TIME 97 minutes
RELEASED 1979
PRODUCED BY Avco Embassy

55   The Mirror Crack'd

DIRECTOR Guy Hamilton
SCENARIO Jonathan Hales, Barry Sandler. Based on a book by Agatha Christie
PHOTOGRAPHY Christopher Challis

EDITOR Richard Marden
CAST Angela Lansbury, Wendy Morgan, Margaret Courtenay, Charles Gray, Maureen Bennet, Carolyn Pickles, Eric Dodson, Charles Lloyd-Pack, Richard Pearson, Thick Wilson, Pat Nye, Peter Woodthorpe, Geraldine Chaplin, Tony Curtis, Edward Fox, Rock Hudson, Kim Novak, Elizabeth Taylor, Marella Oppenheim
RUNNING TIME 105 minutes
RELEASED 1980
PRODUCED BY EMI Films Ltd

56   Between Friends (aka Intimate Strangers)

DIRECTOR Lou Antonio
SCENARIO Based on the novel, *Nobody Makes Me Cry*, by Shelly List
CAST Elizabeth Taylor, Carol Burnett, Barbara Bush, Henry Ramler, Bruce Grey, Roddy McDowall
RUNNING TIME 100 minutes
RELEASED 1983
PRODUCED BY Robert Cooper Films/Marion Rees Assoc/List/Estrin Prods/HBO

57   North and South*

DIRECTOR Richard T. Heffron
SCENARIO Based on the Book by John Jakes on American Civil War. Adapted by Paul F. Edwards, Patricia Green, Douglas Heyes, Kathleen A. Shelley
CAST Elizabeth Taylor, Robert Mitchum, Lesley-Ann Down, David Carradine, Patrick Swayze, Kirstie Alley, Robert Guillaume, Gene Kelly, Inga Swenson, James Read, Jean Simmons
RUNNING TIME 110 minutes per episode (UK); 120 minutes per episode (USA)
RELEASED 1984
PRODUCED BY David L. Wolper Production/Warner Bros. TV (USA)

58   Malice In Wonderland*

DIRECTOR Gus Trikonis
SCENARIO Jacqueline Feather, David Seidler. Based on the book, *Hedda and Louella*, by George Eels
CAST Elizabeth Taylor, Jane Alexander, Richard Dysart, Joyce van Patten, Jon Cypher, Leslie Ackerman, Bonnie Bartlett
RUNNING TIME Two versions – 90 minutes (UK – BBC); 120 minutes (USA – CBS)
RELEASED 1985
PRODUCED BY ITC Productions

59   There Must Be a Pony

DIRECTOR Joseph Sargent
SCENARIO Matt Crowley. Based on the novel by James Kirkwood
CAST Elizabeth Taylor, Robert Wagner, James Coco, William Windom, Edward Winter, Ken Olin

RUNNING TIME   120 minutes
RELEASED   1986
PRODUCED BY RJ Productions and Columbia Pictures

60   Poker Alice*

DIRECTOR   Arthur Allen Seidelman
SCENARIO   James Lee Barrett
CAST   Elizabeth Taylor, George Hamilton, Tom Skerritt, Richard Mulligan, David Wayne, Pat Corley
RUNNING TIME   120 minutes
RELEASED   1987
PRODUCED BY Harvey Matofsky/New World TV

61   Young Toscanini (provisional title)

DIRECTOR   Franco Zeffirelli
TO BE RELEASED   1989

* Denotes films made for television.

Elizabeth Taylor also appeared in a 1942 short, *Man or Mouse*, directed by Jules White; as an extra in *Quo Vadis?* (1951), directed by Mervyn Le Roy; and made guest appearances in *General Hospital* (1981) and *Hotel* (1986) for television.

Stage Plays

1   The Little Foxes by Lillian Hellman (1981)

DIRECTOR   Austin Pendleton
CAST   Elizabeth Taylor, Maureen Stapleton, Anthony Zerbe, Joe Ponazecki, Dennis Christopher, Novella Nelson, Joe Seneca, Humbert Astredo, Ann Talman, Tom Aldredge

2   Private Lives by Noël Coward (1983)

DIRECTOR   Milton Katselas
CAST   Richard Burton, John Cullum, Kathryn Walker, Helena Carroll

Acknowledgements

The author wishes to thank Stephen Sondheim and the copyright holders for permission to quote a lyric from his *Follies*, and Sally Hibbin for her filmography.

The publishers wish to thank the following copyright holders for their permission to reproduce illustrations supplied:
BBC Hulton Picture Library p. 61 (right), 66, 93, 129 (left and right); Camera Press Limited p. 16 (right), 177, 183; The Keystone Collection p. 113 (left), 171; Popperfoto p. 58, 61 (left), 110, 113 (right); The Press Association p. 180 (right); Rex Features p. 17, 180 (left); Topham Picture Library p. 137.

The publishers also wish to thank the following film production and distribution companies whose publicity pictures appear in this book:
ABC; Avco–Embassy; British Film Institute; Cornelius Creem/Cinerama; Columbia; Ernest Lehman; Filmways; General Continental/Harlech TV; Horizon; Huston-Stark; Joseph E Levine; Kastner-Ladd-Kanter; Maximilian-Trianon; MGM; Nassau Film; Oxford University Screen Productions; Paramount; Rank; Rizzolifilm; Royal Films International; Sagittarius; Stevens-Kohlmar; Timon; Twentieth Century Fox; United Artists; Universala; Venfilm; Warner Brothers; World Film Services–Heller; Zeefilm.